M000085300

# Delicate Men
# [stories]

R Dean Johnson

## Praise for *Delicate Men:*

"*Delicate Men* takes a hard look at men caught in that land between here and there, men on the move, men on the verge of what comes next. The writing is sure, and the stories ring true with hard-earned wisdom."

—Lee Martin, Pulitzer Prize Finalist author of *The Bright Forever*

"What's so compelling about R Dean Johnson's Delicate Men is the startling revelation that the anxieties and insecurities of our youth—the ones we are certain we will outgrow—actually haunt us into maturity. Johnson seeks out the pressure points in a range of masculine narratives and shapes a complex portrait of male identity, in which vulnerability begets strength, where desire never gets less awkward, and adults still stand foolishly by playground rules: 'It's a boy's game, but you have to be a man to play it.' Sensitively rendered, Delicate Men is honest and poignant storytelling."

—Rigoberto González, author of *Autobiography of My Hungers*

"These delicate men with their still-soft hearts make their way through machismo and disillusionment, armed with maps of Brugge or nightly tips from valet jobs or white-collar plans for the future, but their delicacy threatens to spoil the fun. R Dean Johnson has given us this sweet gift of good men on the verge of indelicacy. What you'll remember most—besides the storytelling finesse—is how Johnson renders the delicate or fragile space between innocence and culpability."

—Jennifer Spiegel, author of *Love Slave* and *The Freak Chronicles*

"The men in *Delicate Men* are delicate men, yes, in the now-fashionable crisis-of-masculinity sense, but they are also vagabonds and romantics and at times profoundly indelicate men, their indelicateness exposed for all the world to see, and we (the world) are better for having seen them through the tender prism of these mischievous stories by R Dean Johnson."

–Jeff Parker, author of *Ovenman* and *Where Bears Roam the Streets*

"R Dean Johnson's tales of contemporary male rituals and relationship politics never fail to dazzle with their clarity, nuance, and peril, coiled and waiting to strike. It's a minefield out there, where love and career await, and Johnson's heroes try to walk safely through it all, armed only with their hard-won insights and good but fallible hearts. A splendid collection by any measure."

—Wilton Barnhardt, *New York Times* bestselling author of *Lookaway, Lookaway*

Alternative Book Press
2 Timber Lane
Suite 301
Marlboro, NJ 07746
www.alternativebookpress.com

This is a work of fiction. All characters appearing in this work are fictitious. Any resemblance to real people, living or dead or otherwise, or locales is purely coincidental.

2014 Paperback Edition
Copyright 2014 © R Dean Johnson
Cover Illustration by CL Smith
Author's photo by John R. McQuiston
Book Design by Alternative Book Press
All rights reserved
Published in the United States of America by Alternative Book Press
Originally published in electronic form in the United States by Alternative Book Press.

Publication Data
R Dean, Johnson, [2014]
Delicate Men: Stories/ by R Dean Johnson—1st ed.
p. cm.
1. General (Fiction). I Title.
PS1-3576.D43J646    2014
813'.6—dc23

ISBN 978-1-940122-26-7
Printed in the United States of America
10  9  8  7  6  5  4  3  2  1

For Julie,
my best friend, my love,
and the light in everything I do

# Contents

Part I.

**No Better**
Zane - Hollywood, California (2009)
<u>7</u>
**The People We Were**
Jim - Munich, Germany (1994)
<u>9</u>
**A Second Delay**
Colin - Lawrence, Kansas (1996)
33

Part II.

**Delicate Men**
Colin - Pasadena, California (1981)
<u>46</u>
**Something Good**
Garrett - Pasadena, California (1979)
<u>58</u>
**Captain of the Drive**
Paige - Anaheim, California (2002)
61

Part III.

**Cards for All Occasions**
Erik - Laguna Beach, California (2007)
<u>90</u>
**Bluff**
Mark - Atlantic City, New Jersey (2005)
<u>122</u>
**Beginner's Guide to Brugge**
Jim - Brugge, Belgium (1994)
126

<u>Part I.</u>
**No Better** | Zane (2009)

Outside *The Palace* just before 2:00 a.m., just before the club closes, and I'm leaning against a car, my date leaning against me, waiting. The Capital Records building is right there across the street, a stack of deli plates reaching up into a marine layer that's been planning all day to creep in from the coast. It's not a good place to wait, but it's not our car and God knows where Liam has snuck off to. The last I saw, he'd cornered this touchy, grinning girl while his date was in the bathroom. He could be anywhere. Doing anything.

A homeless guy comes weaving across the street, headed for us. I don't have my hands on any change; really, all I want to do is lean against the car and cool off from all the dancing and loud talking over the songs I didn't want to dance to. I'm wearing a brand new shirt and a pair of pants that only come out on weekends, only at night. Who'd believe I don't have a dollar? So I peer into my wallet like it's a darkened room and pull a buck from between two twenties. "That's all I got left, man. There's more ATM receipts in there than bills."

"I hear that," the bum says and takes the buck.

After he leaves and word gets out, another bum comes over to us. "Let me get this one," my date says, a brunette, a really nice girl whose name I'm trying not to remember since this is it, the last time I'll see her because I'm not ready for a nice girl.

She's excited and cuts off his pitch about the war and his veteran's benefits running out. She holds out the dollar like it's an award, like the guy just won a Grammy or something.

The bum stares at the bill. "A dollar? What the fuck am I going to do with a dollar?" She looks like she might cry, her eyes welling up a little and sparkling like her skirt, so I throw an arm around her. She drops her head to search through her little, leather purse for another dollar, or maybe a five, and the bum glances at me without moving his head. He takes a deep breath and his eyes follow the silent exhale to the pavement, and I know it's an apology. He had to try it. He knows I've been paying all night. Knows she must have some money. It would be stupid if he didn't try. And as a few more bucks come out I pull my date a little closer, firm but not intimate, and nod to him, let him know it's okay and that, really, I'm no better.

### The People We Were | Jim (1994)

Two days ago I was leaving Amsterdam for the last time. It was a midweek train so I had no problem finding a quiet car, one with some German families and only three Americans—young guys in their khakis and college T-shirts.

There were farms and pastures filling the windows when one of the Americans came up the aisle to me. I expected him to ask where I was from. It's what Americans do when they think you're from the States or somewhere that seems like an ally, somewhere like Canada or Australia. But this guy had no idea what I was. He raised his eyebrows and flashed a half-grin, some kind of international "Hello." Then he asked me, *Sprechen sie englisch?*

I responded the way Europeans who speak English often do, by answering his question with a question: "What can I do for you?"

He'd been holding his left forearm with his right hand, and he released it just long enough to show me a small cut so fresh it nearly dripped blood on my hands. "Ah," I said, reaching for the Band-Aids in my backpack. He took the one I offered and asked for two more, the way a lot of young Americans leaving Amsterdam do, just the way Eislan said it would be.

Americans have a look, Eislan liked to tell me. *Not innocent*, she'd say, *inferior. Like a cattle.* We met in Amsterdam at Wolvenstraat

Hostel, one of those places that comes with a free breakfast so the bunk-bed in the crowded barrack seems more tolerable. But she wasn't a tourist. Every morning at a quarter past seven, fifteen minutes after breakfast was supposed to start, Eislan would appear behind the counter separating the kitchen from the common room (a basement with old couches and coffee tables made out of crates). By seven-thirty the room would be full, twenty or thirty people groggy and restless, most of them only up this early because it was the day they were leaving, the rest just getting back from the night before. It didn't matter to Eislan, though. She'd take her time, smoothing her apron, tying back her hair and putting everything in order before cracking the first egg. You could say anything you liked, that you were catching a train or suffered from low blood sugar, but you wouldn't eat until she decided.

Back home, I never took the time to eat breakfast. But for three straight mornings, I found myself waiting for Eislan to arrive. I'd let people who were running late go ahead of me, and when I stepped up to order, I'd wait until she looked up. Until we made eye contact. On the third day, Eislan spoke before looking up: *Scrambled eggs, no cheese.* I nodded and she sat a steaming cup atop the counter: *Café American.* She raised her head, grinning, a line on each cheek revealing itself, each forming a slight dimple. *No sugar*, she said, *but cream.* I walked away smiling and speechless. The cream and sugar were self-serve, on a table at the other end of the room.

I signed on for an extra night at the hostel, wished the day away, then wondered the next morning if I'd made a mistake. Chatty English teenagers surrounded me, overflowing from the couches to the crates, the crates to the floor. Their chaperones stood nearby, tapping their watches and glaring at Eislan. This, it suddenly became clear, was my chance. I charged the counter, telling Eislan I could jump back there and help out. She shook her head no and drew me closer with her hand. I could make out each freckle sprinkled about her nose, see wisps of brown hair escaping her braid and contrasting with the light blue of her eyes.

*Your ancestors are in your cheekbones*, she whispered. *Do you know this?*

I smiled, though I had no idea what she meant. Not until that afternoon, in the flat she shared with three other people, would I begin to understand. She dragged me through the front door, pulling me down to the couch and telling me we'd have to make love right then before her roommates got home, right there because the living room was her room, and the couch was her bed. Later, as we lay wrapped in a blanket stolen, she said, from her own parents, she lightly traced my cheekbones with her fingers, telling me they were very European and beautiful, not diluted like most Americans. I took the compliment, happy to accept it as truth so long as it meant being with her.

Eislan wanted me to understand Amsterdam as she did. She took me places I said I'd already seen, making me leave my camera behind the second time. She said cameras filter you from reality. Reality, she showed me, was bringing a loaf of bread to the Anne Frank House, tearing off chunks and offering it to the tourists in the long line outside. The gesture unnerves some people, I do not know exactly why, but Eislan told me that was our plan. *This is not Disneyland*, she said. *No one in that line should feel comfortable.*

We avoided the Van Gogh Museum altogether, instead walking the cobblestone streets he walked, crossing over wooden foot bridges and gazing into the dark canal water to see our reflections—distinct at first, then distorting in gentle waves brought on by the breeze or maybe a duck beneath the bridge. Our stroll took us to the Jordaan, a quieter part of the city with narrow streets and block after block of vine-laden, five-story buildings. Merchants and professional offices occupied the first floors with apartments rising above, peaking through the vines and capped with sloped roofs. On one of the few streets in the city with any kind of pitch, Eislan led me to a building distinguished from its neighbors only by the yellow trim around the windows. She said the Van Gogh family briefly occupied an apartment in this building, though which one is not known for certain. Then she pointed out the two windows on the fourth floor she

thought it might be.  How could she know, I
asked, and she said the family who lived there
now were oppressive and cruel, and they have
been for years. *Like a curse*, she said. I'd like
to have known more, but she kissed me just
then, and I let it go.

A few streets over was the Prins Saarein,
a pub hidden half way down the block, the
sign so small and dimly lit only a local would
know it wasn't some newsstand closed for the
day. The ceilings were low and stained a pale
brown, years of smoke from cigarettes and who
knows what else. A friend of Eislan's spotted
us through the haze, waving us over to his
table, insisting we join him.  Ruud said he
hadn't seen Eislan around in a while. *I have
not been around*, she said.  He nodded as
though he'd forgotten, then asked what I was
drinking.  When I said Heineken he smiled,
and I did not know if it was because I ordered
wrong or if drinking the local beer meant I was
trying too hard.  Eislan ordered the same,
though, and Ruud asked if she'd have
something more, his treat. *I'm fine with just
beer*, she said. It reassured me the way she
extended herself to protect me, the way she
whispered halfway through the pint how I
should get her out of there, get her back to the
hostel and down to the small toilet hidden
near the kitchen where we could make love
standing up.

Two days later, when I reached the
maximum stay at Wolvenstraat Hostel, I found
a backpacker's inn with weekly rates.  It was
closer to Eislan's flat, and I surprised her

there that afternoon with two tickets for a big concert. For a band she loved. *But when is the show?* she said.

I tapped the date printed on the tickets. "Next month," I said.

Eislan held me for a moment in her gaze, then she pulled me into the living room, leaving the door wide open and kissing me hard.

She had me; she must have known. She began speaking of Americans and other tourists with disdain, insisting I wasn't like them and kissing me in pubs and in front of outdoor cafes to prove it. Later that week, on the night she spoke of expanding her horizons, of invading the countryside, she must have been certain that I'd volunteer to join her, that I'd rush back to my room, strap on my pack and meet her at Centraal Station without asking where we were going or if we'd return in time for the concert.

We found a couchette all to ourselves and lay in the dark planning our getaway, first to Munich for fun, then to Switzerland when our money ran out. She knew of a hostel where we could find work. It would all work out, she said.

Early the next morning, when I woke to the sight of Eislan leaning over a waste basket with a syringe stuck in her arm, I let her calm me down with a story about her lifelong battle with diabetes, and I chose to believe her.

Everything felt perfect those first hours in Munich: the intimate crowds in the pubs; the camaraderie of strangers singing together in beer gardens; the bike rides between and the freedom to go where we wanted, when we wanted. I realized I was now a month past my severance pay and into my savings, but I was conquering a foreign city on a rented bicycle with my Dutch lover. No matter how much I scoured the *L.A. Times* classifieds, I could never find that. And even if there were plenty of listings under "investment banking," none of them are honest. They don't tell you what it's really like to be a junior associate. It's long hours that keep you away from your girlfriend so much she thinks you take her for granted, thinks she has to cheat on you to get your attention. It's a cubicle in a smog-encircled skyscraper where you run numbers and determine risk, deny loans and kill the dreams of people you only meet on paper. And when things aren't going well for the company, you find out you're a faceless name too, just another number to be cut.

With Eislan, I could bury my recent past in a beer garden, smooth it over singing oom-pa-pa songs. With Eislan, I only need look two weeks into the future, when I'd be in the Swiss Alps scrubbing bathrooms. *Good, clean work*, she said.

As the day waned and the light left us, Eislan grew nervous atop her bicycle, completely losing confidence anytime asphalt gave way to decorative cobblestone. *It's not like home*, she said. *We don't have so many cars.* She felt out of control, as if she'd slip and be trampled by a stampede of

Volkswagens and Audis. She'd swerve towards the curb every time a car rumbled by until finally a curb, not a car, got her. We didn't know her ankle and wrist had literally broken her fall until the next morning when our buzzes wore off.

The German doctor set both casts quickly, offered Eislan the state-approved pharmaceuticals, then said, quietly, he could get her something a little stronger that would have her feeling much better much sooner. She turned everything down, even the free stuff, and assured me that she didn't really need a crutch, just time.

We stayed drunk for two days, until Eislan discovered alcohol makes a poor pain killer. Trips to the bathroom were too frequent, and throwing up anywhere but next to the bed was impossible.

At the follow-up appointment, the doctor told Eislan the casts wouldn't come off for six weeks. He asked her how she was handling the pain and suggested the meds again, either kind. We lingered in the examination room, arguing over getting her some pain relief until I gave up, and we fell silent. We listened to the hum of the fluorescent lights overhead. I stared at a row of glass jars on the counter: tongue depressors, cotton swabs, and adhesive bandages. It took me a moment before I realized the bandages were labeled in English, "Band-Aid." I smiled and stole a handful, telling Eislan we should have something to show for all the time we'd lost in this place. She laughed and let me help her to her feet, let me win the meds argument, though only the stronger stuff so she could be through with it quicker.

Outside in the parking lot, we couldn't buy as much as the doctor suggested; the trunk of his Mercedes didn't come with a credit card machine. Instead, he took the little money Eislan had and as much of mine as he could find. Eislan assured me it would be fine, that she may not even use it all anyway.

After the wounded American on the train thanked me for all three Band-Aids, he walked immediately to the toilette, only stopping by his seat to grab a backpack and tell his two friends everything was going to be fine.

It was nearly nine o'clock when the train crossed into Germany, the late dusk behind us pushing west, purple descending on the trees as the sun surrendered to night. The three Americans started playing cards, trying to act natural as the German conductor came aboard at the first station. He was emotionless when asking for tickets, passports, papers, anything he needed to understand who you were and what you were about. He looked the Americans over and gave them no trouble. I know they thought they'd made it then. They slumped back in their seats, abandoning the card game in favor of talk, all the sights they'd see in Munich, all the beer they'd drink and the women they'd meet. They laughed and rambled on, interrupting each other, speaking as though nothing but good times and glory lay ahead.

On the outskirts of Cologne, the train stopped and German police stormed the cars. The Americans sat straight up, shocked at the rumble of boots as half a dozen officers ran down the aisle, two stationing themselves at the end, the rest pushing on. A captain followed them aboard, walking casually and politely asking for I.D.'s and destinations. I'd seen this once before. Eislan warned me it could happen and taught me how to avoid detention. *Sit with a German newspaper folded up small*, she said. *That's the way the young German guys do it. They look bored, annoyed they have to look away from football scores to show I.D.* It works too. The officers barely glance at those guys, almost as if they're apologizing for the inconvenience.

I'd left my passport out on the table in front of me, half buried amongst cassette tapes and my Walkman. When the captain settled his black leather boots at my feet, I looked him in the eye and addressed him with the little German I know. I'd done this once before, and I felt fine until I noticed they'd brought a dog aboard.

The funny thing about smuggling drugs into Germany is that the best place to hide them is somewhere on or near yourself—in a money belt or a backpack. The police usually snoop around the empty seats and luggage bins; they only violate your personal space if you look nervous. But dogs can smell what the police cannot see, and when the captain responded to my *Guten abend* with a glance at my unzipped backpack, I'm certain it looked conspicuous.   It might have been fine for everyone if I hadn't glanced at the bag myself, but as soon as I did he lost all interest in pleasantries or anything I had sitting out on the table.  So I apologized for not knowing how to say it in German, then pointed to the three Americans and explained how I'd given one of them three bandages for a tiny cut.   The captain understood completely.   *Danka,* he said, then lead the officer with the dog over to the three Americans.

They stared at his sidearm, his boots, his badge, everywhere but his eyes.  They couldn't understand his command to hand over their backpacks and nearly jumped when he started grabbing them himself.   The dog sniffed all three packs, deeply but without reaction, and the captain looked satisfied.  He began holding up each pack individually and handing it back to the proper owner.   As the wounded American reached for his, the dog caught scent of his hand and exploded, volleys of barking reverberating through the car.   The captain shouted orders and all at once, it died.  He held his hands up, encouraging everyone to relax.  To wait.  The Americans cowered in their seats, and they must have known they were marked.   A moment later, an officer emerged from the toilette with a baggy of hash, the Band-Aids that held it under the sink or behind the waste basket still attached and sagging over themselves.  The wounded American looked to me for help, his eyes wide open and pleading as the officers stepped in screaming orders, dragging him and his friends from their seats and off the train.

The captain lingered a moment, looking back at me to nod his appreciation, then he left the train without the insult of inspecting my backpack or interrogating me further.

For the record, I am not a drug dealer. Before I met Eislan, I wouldn't smuggle store-bought candy into a movie theater. In fact, when I met the three Americans the day before yesterday, it was only the second time I'd smuggled heroin into Germany.

I did everything I could to help Eislan while we were in Munich. She could barely move without wincing in pain or having to stop altogether. I explained the situation to Georg, a young German who worked at the hostel. Money was tight, I said, and we couldn't leave after three days like you're supposed to because Eislan could hardly get from the bed to the door. He was sympathetic and arranged for me to clean the toilettes and sinks and showers in exchange for the room. He even snuck us some food when he could. As far as the three day rule went, he said if I could cover the front desk for an hour on the nights his girlfriend dropped by for conjugal visits, he could create new names for us every three days and make the register look legitimate. We stopped existing as the people we were, taking on new identities every three days—Sid and Nancy first, then Joe and Marilyn. Nobody really checked, but Georg insisted we be careful.  The least likely person may turn us in, he said. He'd seen it happen before.

Still, my efforts could not change Eislan's plight:  captive in a room barely larger than the bed itself, the only natural light filtering through a thick pane of milky glass.  Even when she could hobble out to the courtyard, things weren't much better.  Just a few rays of sunlight trickled down on to the gravel and the only vegetation was confined to a few potted plants.  It looked gray and cold all the time, only serving to remind her there was no relief in sight.

Eislan broke down on the fifth night, the day after her pain medication ran out.  *It is too much*, she said, and I offered to go back, to get the free stuff.  It would be better than nothing. She shook her head and asked for her backpack, then pulled out the methadone and handed it to me.  She explained her years of heroin abuse, the months she spent in rehab last winter, and the state-supported program she'd been on ever since.  *The doctor could tell what I was*, she said.  *He knew I'd need something stronger.  But everything aches now, not just my ankle and wrist.*

Eislan swore just a few hits would get her right, and I didn't know what she was asking of me at first, not until she rambled on about her friend back in Amsterdam.  Did I remember him? Ruud, from the Prins Saarein, the pub in the Jordaan.  I could trust him, and he could get me more hits than she needed if I traded the concert tickets.  *You can sell the rest*, she said, *I only need a little and you can get a lot more for heroin in Germany than you can in Holland.* I understood then what she wanted from me, but the magnitude of the whole thing was blurred by the way she asked. Could I see that this is not really the person she was? Did I understand that she'd already agonized over this? Couldn't I please just trust her?

We spent a day going over the plan: the best times to find Ruud, how to make the deal, pack the score, and get it on the train. I was on edge the entire trip, expecting at any moment to be recognized for what I was and be detained. But I was not. I returned to Munich near midnight, Hauptbahnhof Station so empty I could hear the echo of my own footsteps as I passed through a corridor into the cavernous main terminal. I emerged from the station into a warm night, feeling festive, as though I'd accomplished something significant and great.

Eislan wanted a fix right away and made me lead her into the bathroom. It takes two hands to shake a little powder from the baggie and on to a spoon, mix it, and heat it with a lighter until it melts. It takes at least one steady hand to suck the junk into a syringe and inject it. Eislan had only one free hand, an unsteady one, so it all fell to me. We went into the showers, just in case there was any blood, and I tried to think of it as an experiment. A life lesson.

With the pain muted, Eislan leaned into me, smiling and pushing us from the bathroom to the courtyard. We kissed for the first time in days, real kisses, and Eislan fantasized of escaping Germany, of walking straight out Centraal Station, turning right and walking the ten minutes to the Jordaan. She'd find the building with the yellow trim and actually go inside this time, actually reunite with her parents. It made her laugh, she said, the way she'd abandoned her family and university studies a year ago thinking them all oppressive. She threw her arms up at the walls in the courtyard, saying nothing could be worse than this. She laughed again, and when we went to bed later that night, she let me make love to her.

The next day, Georg told me how to sell the hits I didn't leave with Eislan. You just put a pen behind your left ear and hang out on the trolley. People come up to you and ask, *Do you have a pen I could borrow?* They actually do it in German first, but if you answer in English they switch to that without a second thought. *How long do you need it for?* They give you a number: *Just one minute, two minutes*, whatever and you know how much they need. *Okay, but I paid fifty Euros for this pen, so I'll need it back.* Some people actually take the pen and pretend to write something. The conductors don't care. They keep their eyes forward and know they'll be safe because a good dealer would never let a junkie roll a conductor. As far as they're concerned, it's a victimless crime.

The day after that first fix, Eislan found her way into a heroin fog. She knew her supply was limited, so she spent the morning concentrating, quietly holding out as long as she could until the next fix. It gave me a chance to slip away with my camera and play tourist. I saw Munich the way a guidebook would tell me to: cathedrals, museums, the Glockenspiel, even the Hofbrauhaus. That night, I gave Eislan a second hit and escaped the next morning in her fog. I found the park where the 1972 Summer Olympics were held. The autobahn runs along one side while office towers and apartment buildings frame the rest of the grounds. It's calculated, carved into the city yet somehow quiet. In the middle of the grounds sits a lake with rolling hills rising from its banks and platoons of trees opening up for footpaths. Gently rising above it all is the Olympic Stadium, its roof a series of sloping, white canvas tents, like a clump of water lilies draped over one another to hide any sharp angles or steel. If I kept my eyes from rising above the roof, concentrated on a bit of blue sky and the tops of trees, the towers standing so alert nearby ceased to exist. Munich hid behind leaves, then floated away with the clouds.

I stayed in the park most of the day, walking the footpaths and taking pictures of the stadium from all angles, trying to capture in film what I could imagine with my eyes. I napped beneath a tree and woke to kids running loose near me in the grass, their parents up on the path standing guard. As I headed for the trolleys, a young guy, too brown to be German, caught up with me and asked to borrow a pen. I was out of heroin by then and not wearing the pen.

"Do I look like a dealer?"

*No,* he said, *but you look like you might know one.* He told me people don't hang around the park that long unless they're up to something. *I have plenty of money,* he said. *We can get high together. My treat.* I said I don't get high, and he said that was best, not to mix business with pleasure. Then he pulled a wad of cash from his pocket, and I said I may know of someone. *Magnificent,* he said, forcing the money into my hand and asking for a day and time to meet.

When I took the money, I thought I'd never see him again. I didn't want to deal, but the next day Eislan begged me to make another score. She promised to do only one hit every other day, to use the methadone in between days, and to get better fast so we could return to Amsterdam. Go back to being the people we were. Then she told me I was her savior.

It was on my second trip to Amsterdam that I crossed paths with the three Americans. I'd packed the heroin into cassette tape cases, the ones I left on the table with my Walkman, out in the open, pushed up against the window and away from the dog.

Outside the train, I could hear the Americans pleading with their captors. It wasn't their hash, they said. *We're just college students; we're not that that kind of people.* A moment later, their pleas were interrupted by the tap of boots growing louder and more frequent, like an approaching rainstorm. I peered out the window as more police arrived. They cleared a path to a tunnel away from the other passengers and began pulling the three Americans toward it. *Okay,* one of the Americans said, *it's ours. But we have money. How much do you want?* I understood what he was doing, I'd have done the same, but it was too late. Things had gone too far.

As the train jerked to movement and began rolling from the station, I watched the three Americans disappear into the tunnel. It was only hash. I can't imagine they got into too much trouble, but I don't know for sure. I only know it just as easily could have been me, and it's not like I wanted to make that choice; I was forced into it.

My return to Munich was even later this time, two in the morning, Hauptbahnhof Station even quieter. On my walk back to the hostel, I passed a few clubs still pulsing with music, people draped over each other, still celebrating the night even though morning had crept up on them.

Georg was asleep behind the desk when I got in. I woke him to get my new name and tell him it was the last we'd need. I paid him up-front, and I apologized for quitting my toilette duties so abruptly. He didn't mind; he'd already gotten someone else while I was gone. *You can always get someone to do your dirty work,* he said.

I crept into the room, slid under the covers with Eislan and placed a hand on her shoulder. It felt smaller than I remembered. She woke and reached across me to click on the lamp, her eyes shadowy and sunken in the dim light. I told her news of the score, and though she smiled only briefly, the lines of her dimples did not seem to go away. Then she insisted I help her hobble into the bathroom for a fix.

It was the last I ever gave her. Later that morning, I paid Georg to do it for me the rest of the time. I showed him where I hid the score, in the cassette cases, then took half of it with me to give to the guy I'd met in the park.

After we made the transaction on a trolley, Salvador insisted we go for a beer. He was a Spaniard, the son of someone important in Bilbao. He shook his head before I could respond, telling me Bilbao was an industrial city and that's why I did not know it. *You don't want to know it*, he said. He spoke of attending university in Pamplona and again shook his head before I could speak. *It is not like you think*, he said. *Only for ten days, when the bulls run, is Pamplona exciting. The rest of the time, no. It is surrounded by nothing. Full of nothing. Campesinos*, he said, flicking his hand as though he were dismissing the entire bar. *Every summer, I escape as soon as I can.*

Salvador admitted he did not do heroin all that much; he just liked to have it with him in the clubs to flash around. After a couple steins, we decided to make a day of it. We found our way back to the Olympic Park so I could show Salvador the way I saw it. I sat him under a tree, directing his focus on the stadium until the giant water lilies appeared and he understood.

*Magnificent*, he said. *You must let me repay you.*

He pulled me aboard a commuter train out of the city and into the Bavarian woods. Salvador said everyone should visit a concentration camp the way he intended us to: high. *We can alter ourselves*, he said, *and play the part of victim.* I said I'd give it a shot, but without altering myself.

As a child, when I learned about places like Dachau, I never imagined them set near quiet villages or surrounded by forests dense with pine—every one of them a perfect Christmas tree. Salvador led me past everything to a corner of the camp opposite the road and front gate, right on the edge of the forest. He thought it made most sense to see the showers first, to work our way back to the guard tower, the barracks and the museum. We paused outside the building, a modest rectangle made of stone. Salvador told me to imagine the long train ride in the crowded cars, the German soldiers screaming at me, pulling me off the train and looking me over, then the simple promise of a shower—the thought of clean walls and smooth floors giving me hope.

*I can see it*, he said, *can you?*

Salvador began sobbing as we stepped inside. The walls were plain, soft with paint and stripped bare of the piping, not nearly as menacing as I would have imagined. His sobs grew stronger, and I put my arm over his shoulder to console him. He quieted, though his entire body convulsed to the point other visitors were noticing, some beginning to sob themselves. I rushed him outside and over by the fence where he could cry it out. It was quiet in that spot, the trees on the other side of the wire and wooden posts not even rustling with a breeze, as if the whole forest was holding its breath until we moved on.

I asked if we should head back to Munich. Salvador raised his hand, stopping me in mid-sentence, and told me when people stumble during Los San Fermines, the worst thing they can do is try to hide from the bulls. *Those are the people who get trapped in a doorway and gored*, he said. *You have to keep running.*

The museum at the front of the camp bustled like an artist's showing. Cubicle walls, with photographs hung every few inches, zigzagged through the center of a long hall. We joined the line of people navigating the maze one moment at a time. These are the photographs you see in high school history books and commemorative issues of *Life Magazine*: emaciated prisoners wearing striped pants and jackets, staring at you with old eyes. Salvador kept hold of his emotions, looking outside on occasion to keep himself grounded.

The middle of the exhibit featured photographs that never made the cut for *Life* or the *Associated Press*: boring shots of the compound or prisoners dead and tangled in barbed wire, suicide under the guise of an escape attempt. Salvador began commenting on every photo, speaking fast and forgetting I do not know Spanish. At the end of one aisle was a photo of five men standing at roll call. Four of them looked past me, over the cubicles and out the windows, beyond the reconstructed barrack and off into the forest. The fifth man stared at me, a slight, almost imperceptible grin upon his face. I may not have noticed if his colleagues weren't so void of expression, making his face seem lively, almost animated. Along with the four others, he had been picked out for the camp's g-force experiment because he looked fit and strong; the experiment would not kill him right away. It would kill him though, a series of photos down the next aisle confirmed that. I followed along as they strapped him in a seat attached to a large gyro. The photos grew increasingly blurry as his eyes squeezed tighter, his cheeks fluttered, and his lips curled back, revealing clenched teeth. Not until the final photo did clarity return. His head rested to one side, blood trickling from his ears, nose and mouth. Here it was half a century later, and even in black and white, even dead, he looked young and healthy.

As Salvador disappeared around the next corner, I stopped to look outside, to calm myself the way he had been doing. I could see beyond all the gravel rectangles set in rows like gardens, back to a time when barracks, not weeds, rose from the ground. I recognized the entire place—the hard-pack dirt road, the gate, the guard towers, the bend in the fence out by the showers—it was the background in all those photographs, all just outside.

Salvador and I rode back to Munich in silence and departed without making plans for the evening. It was ten minutes to five when I arrived at the hostel, ten minutes before it would reopen. I crept around back, the way Georg had shown me, expecting to surprise Eislan in the room. Instead I found my pack on the bed, cassette tape cases spilling out and scattered about the unmade blankets. I walked to the toilette, hearing the echo of voices and laughter before I got to the door. She was in there with Georg, probably in the shower stabbing for a fresh vein or experimenting with different doses. I don't know for sure; I never looked. I went back to the room and gathered my pack—clothes, towel, money—everything except the cassettes. I left them where they lay, even the ones that had nothing but music in them, and headed for Hauptbahnhof, for the first train out of Germany.

In Stuttgart, after I had time to think about where I wanted to be, I changed to the train I'm on now. I'm going to Pamplona, then out to the countryside beyond so I can see what it's like the other fifty-one weeks of the year, when the bulls are left alone in the fields to graze, and play, and ponder the best place to take a nap—long before they're herded into a pen, transported into the city, and sent running down cobblestone streets to see who gets hurt first.

## A Second Delay | Colin (1996)

It was fall in ways I hadn't experienced since I was a kid—crisp air and crunchy leaves on the sidewalk. Patrick and I were out from California to visit Jim, still in the first semester of his starving artist experiment.

Jim took us to the street where all the cool kids hung out, to the Aqua Lounge, a dark chamber lit only by the fish tanks embedded in the velvet walls. It was four in the afternoon and empty except for the band setting up in the other room and the bartender, a woman with short, bleach blonde hair. "She looks like an actress," Jim whispered, as if that somehow legitimized his moving away from us.

Patrick waited until she stepped away, off to some secret room for cocktail napkins, then nailed it: "A young, Meg Ryan. Like, *Top Gun* era, Meg Ryan." Patrick works in Century City, in one of those towers that looks like a giant roll of pennies. His firm handles actors and models, just contracts and visas, things like that, no murder trials or kiddie porn defenses. But he plays the entertainment biz card all the time, for fun mostly, because as good as it sounds at clubs and parties, Patrick's been glued to the same girlfriend for three years.

We sat single-file at the bar, Jim in the middle so we could grill him from both sides. "We're buying," I said, "now that you're a poor college student again."

Meg Ryan handed us each a drink menu. Without looking, Jim ordered a classic, shaken not stirred.  Patrick went with a Manhattan. Then it was my turn and something that had chocolate liqueur leapt out at me.  I was drinking in the middle of a Thursday afternoon, why not?

Jim couldn't handle it. "I bring you to the best martini bar in Lawrence and you order that!"

It had to be the only martini bar in Lawrence.  Maybe the only one in Kansas.  I held up the laminated menu.  "It's a real martini.  Look."

Patrick shook his head.  "Why don't you just order a milkshake?"

Meg Ryan took the menu from me. "Don't listen to them," she said. "It's a good drink."

I nodded like, "See," and thanked her.

We had two more rounds while Meg put us all on trial:  We were too old to be undergrads, too well-dressed to be regular grad students, so who were we?  Did we all go to law school, or just me and Patrick?  Was it really that hard?  "And Jim," she said like he'd slapped her ass, "How can you leave all that investment banking money for, what was it, an MFA in Mixed Media?  What the Hell does that even mean?"  That's what Patrick and I wanted to know, so we loved Meg for saying it.  For the way she said it.  Meg in her ribbed, wife-beater T and cutoff jean shorts.  Meg keeping up with the conversation while prepping the bar for the night—leaning against it to talk, across it to clean, stretching out to put glasses and bottles in place, bending down and over to pick up things, unseen things, from beneath the bar.

We knew what she was doing. We'd seen it before in Santa Monica, Silver Lake, Westwood, where ever. It worked all over So Cal. Of course it would work in Kansas. She made more from us in an hour than she probably would the rest of the night when the real college students started clogging up the place.

We were old enough to know hanging out with the bartender at four, then five in the evening, was far from cool, so we left for dinner. And me, I was drunk on what turned out to be pretty good martinis, drunk on Meg, drunk on the idea of those days when you didn't have to be anywhere on a weekday, even class.

\*

The guy I interned for after law school told me that you don't really have to make a career decision until you turn thirty. Unless you have kids. We left Jim at the airport in Kansas City with a smile on his face and a year to spare.

When we got back to L.A., Patrick found out the tests were still positive. He could decide if he wanted to be a husband or not, but he was definitely going to be a father.

I came home to my new condo, my new furniture, my new kitchen with the view of the ocean and the new espresso maker right there on the counter next to the envelope with my copy of the divorce papers inside. It felt like I'd made a career decision. It felt that way the minute she said we should try for a baby and I said we should try to be happy first. It was the wrong thing to say, and the right one, and it was a decision. None of it felt good, but it was honest.

*

I'm flying home through Kansas City on a Friday, maybe a month later. A last minute thing and I don't tell Jim because I'll only be there to change planes, why make him drive the hour in from Lawrence to see me for five minutes? Then there's the mechanical difficulty and a delay, and a second delay, and then a different plane that never shows and I land on a list of people with a free hotel room and a flight in the morning. Suddenly, I want a martini and the cab fare to Lawrence doesn't seem like it would be all that much.

When I get to the Aqua Lounge, the place is packed because some band that makes Kansans go crazy is playing tonight. There's even a cover charge. I slip my tie into my pocket and get a story ready for Meg, that I'm supposed to meet Jim, has she seen him, does she remember him, or maybe me? Later, I'll see if she wants to go somewhere quiet, maybe a late dinner, maybe her place or if she has roommates to navigate, my hotel room. Whatever works. I'm buying.

Meg is standing by the bar, but on the customer side. I walk up like she's not there, look past her to the bartender. A martini seems complicated now. Somehow wrong. So I order a beer. Two beers. One for me and one for my friend. The one who isn't really here.

"Hey, California," Meg says. "You here with your friends?"

I look at her too fast.   Then too long. She's in cuffed jeans and a checkered shirt tied up at her bellybutton ring; her hair up like Madonna, or Marilyn Monroe; her lips a bright red.  It's like nothing in California right now, a style ahead or behind the times, but she makes it look good.  "Yeah, I'm supposed to meet the one who lives here now.  Have you seen him?"

She rounds her eyes, shakes her head.

"Are you working?" I say.

"Nah," she says.  "I'm just so pathetic I hang out here on my nights off."

I nod.  I don't know why.  To agree that she's pathetic?

The beers arrive and I open a tab, lay a tip on the bar too, just to make it clear I'm worth the attention.  I look to the swinging doors on the left, past them to the room with the stage where, I say, I'll be if she happens to see Jim before I do.  "You don't mind telling him, right?"

She doesn't mind.

"Thanks," I say.  "See ya later."

"When?" she says, and I stop.  "There's something I want to ask you about."  She's looking right at me.  Serious.  She means it.

I glance at the doors, the doors I'm going to walk through and find my friend who really isn't there, give him the real beer I bought for him.  "The band won't be on too soon, will they?"

Meg shrugs.  Smiles.

"Let me find Jim and if there's time, I'll come back before the first set. Or maybe between sets. You'll be here?"

She taps the bar. "Right here, stealing toothpicks and cherries."

*

The concert hall is more like a gymnasium, wide with a wooden floor and no seats. It's cluttered with groups of over-dressed fans, blazers and fishnets and ripped concert T's from the tours before this one that prove whose loved them longest and most. The balcony is full, and why am I even looking up there? Jim isn't here, and even if he is I don't want to see him. I'll take the first, sad-looking undergrad I see and float him a free beer.

It turns out to be a little guy in a tight polo, collar up, some kind of rune on the stone dangling from his neck and arms so white they're translucent in the stage lights. He's standing alone, staring at the dark stage. "Here," I say. "It's on the house."

He takes the beer and turns his head sideways. "Is this a trick?"

"No trick," I say. "I had an extra and you looked like you could use a beer."

He can't hide his smile. "I can. But I don't normally take drinks from strange men."

It makes me feel old for an instant.

"Whatever," I say. "You can set it down if you like."

The lights drop and I turn to make my exit. The stage glows behind me and everyone in the back of the room surges forward. I turn sideways, raise my arms bullfighter style, but there's no threading through. I'm pushed backwards, headed for the stage, and turn in time to see the lead singer, long shorts, boots and dreads, leaning into the crowd as the drums roll. He's high-fiving everyone, including me.

\*

Meg isn't at the bar after the set, and I wonder how hard it is to catch a cab in this town. I'm sweaty from the mosh pit, my suit jacket at my side. I'm kind of proud of how it all came back to me, though. I even threw the kid in the tight polo on my shoulders for a song, then lost him when he jumped on stage.

A good, head-clearing piss is in order. Then I should cut my losses, settle up, and leave.

There's a line. The hallway is narrow so you've got to hug the wall to hold your place, to show you're not just passing through.

I'm hugging my balled-up suit jacket, staring at my feet when some cuffed jeans stop in front of me. It's Meg, maybe three inches from my face. "California," she says.

I want to say, "Meg." I don't. "That's a pretty good band," I say.

"Everybody loves *The Urge*," she says, no hint of irony, no chance it's a come-on.

The line moves but I don't, so the guy next to me needs to know: "Standing or pissing?"

I wave him around me and ask Meg, "You need a drink?"

She holds a glass up to my face, clinking the ice.

"Right," I say.

"You got a minute?" she says.

"Two," I say.

She looks sideways. "Not here. Come on."

Meg leads me through the doors, back into the concert hall, into the shadows of an amp stack near the stage. She slides a porcelain cigarette out of her front jean pocket and starts packing it, I don't ask with what. Then, she hands it to me, her lighter trailing. "Want to do a one-hitter?"

After a few drags, the smoke clouding around us, she smiles and takes back the cigarette. She looks me over and I'm sure my suit is saying things I don't want it to say about me. "Your friend sent me a post card."

"Jim?" I say.

"That wasn't the name. The other guy from California."

"Patrick," I say, and she squints, nods a little, not totally sure but it has to be him.

"He sent it here, to 'The Meg Ryan Bartender.' I got so much shit for that."

"Sorry," I say.

"He wanted me to call him at his office." She's almost yelling now, to be heard more so than out of anger. But there's some of that too. "What's wrong with that guy?"

"He was having a bit of a crisis. He's okay now."

Meg puts an arm on the wall next to my head and leans forward, "Are you having a crisis too?"

It's either a come-on or an interrogation. Maybe both, I can't tell. So I just go with the truth, even if it isn't the whole truth and nothing but: "I'm passing though.   On business."

She looks me over before pushing back off the wall. "That's it?"

I shrug. "That's it."

She squints, then grins, then nods. "Wait here."

I'm thinking she might be going to get her purse or something she's stashed behind the bar.   Then she'll ask if I want to get out of here.   It's going to be her apartment.   I'm wondering now if there are roommates to account for. I should've called Jim.

Meg returns with a friend at her side—the little man in the tight polo. "This is Kendall."

I hold up a hand, give him a slight wave. "We've met."

Meg's eyes go round.   "And?"

"He gave me a beer," says Kendall.

I put my hand on his shoulder, like we're tight.   "We sort of danced too," I say, and Kendall smiles, confirming it for Meg.

She turns to me.   "You never found your friend?"

"No," I say.   "I found Kendall."

He smiles at Meg.

She nods, smiles.   She puts one hand on my shoulder, one on Kendall's.   "I'll be right back, guys."

She steps away, gliding around clumps of people until she's meshed with all the other arms and legs.   The hair and jewelry.   The darkness.

I turn to see Kendall has been watching me watch her. He looks like a client, attentive, waiting for me to say just the right thing. I throw a thumb back towards Meg. "You think she's coming back?"

Kendall shrugs. He doesn't seem concerned. I look to the back of the room again. To the doors. Why did she leave? And why would she drag this little man over to me and then go? I look back at Kendell and his eyes are waiting for me like dinner on the table.

Oh.

He takes a breath, says, "You want to get out of here?"

"Yeah." I slide on my jacket. "I should get going."

Kendall looks happy. Relieved. "Okay," he nods.

"Alone," I say.

"Oh, yeah," he says, nodding too fast. A closed-mouth smile scribbles itself across his face. It wavers and won't stick, so he turns his head sideways.

I can leave now. It's not the first time I've made a mistake. Sometimes things look so promising at first, easy, open and shut, then they don't work out. It happens. You cut your losses and move on. I'll be fine. And I don't have to explain anything to this kid I'll never see again. I can just get a cab and go back to my life.

"Listen," I say, and I'm not sure why I'm bothering to say it, why I'm excusing myself before I go. "I think I gave you the wrong impression. I'm not gay."

He turns to me. "I didn't think you were gay."

"Yeah you did." I'm certain of this and I'm not going to deal in anything but truth. There's nothing to lose here. No angle. "Come on. I gave you a beer? Said I danced with you?" He stares at me, evaluates the evidence. "And did, um, did she—" I point to the back of the room, not knowing what to call Meg since that really isn't her name.

"Tracy," Kendall says.

"Tracy. Did Tracy tell you I'm from California?"

He nods.

"So, that too. Everyone in California is gay, right?" I smile. "Honest mistake."

Kendall nods, smiles a little. "I'm sorry."

"No, man," I shake my head. He isn't getting this. "I'm the one who's sorry. It was my fault, not yours."

If I were back home, I'd definitely go now. But I can linger, be human without having to explain to my friends that that's all this is. That it's okay to want to do this.

"I'm Colin," I say and put out a hand.

Kendall shakes it and it seems we have an understanding now.

"Got any good burrito places around here?"

Kendall nods.

"Come on," I say and flick my head towards the doors. "I'm buying."

*

We walk along Massachusetts Avenue, music pumping from the bars and clubs, college kids in threes and fours. Kendell's arms are plunged into his barn coat and with its ripped pocket and faded spots, it looks like it came out of a real barn, not a catalogue. I'm hugging myself, the late Kansas fall more biting than a deep Southern California winter.

Finally, we're there. A tiny, walk-up, drive-up place called Burrito King. No lobby. No relief from the cold. I have my doubts this burrito will be anything close to an actual burrito, but there's a line of cars and a smattering of people standing around, eating.

The guy at the window has on a Dodgers hat, the white, interlocked L.A. like a beacon. Kendall orders for us, I pay, and the guy in the hat sounds authentically East L.A.

"You from So Cal?" I say.

"Riverside," he says.

Close enough. I wonder if Jim has found this place yet. I should've called him. What kind of friend am I?

Kendall and I stand in the cold and wait. He tells me about school, the farm community he grew up in, all the places he'll go and the things he's going to do after graduation. He can't wait to start. I listen and say little. It's nice to hear his excitement.

I don't know exactly how cold it's gotten, how cold I've become, until Kendell hands me my burrito. It's steaming in the night air and so big I have to take it with two hands. It's wide and heavy, swaddled in plain, white paper.

Kendall digs in like he hasn't eaten since the last time he was home.  He pauses after a few bites, noticing the burrito laying across my hands, tingling them back to life.  He smiles and wipes his face.  "You can eat it," he says. "It's not a baby."

"I know."  I laugh, a real one, and he does too, but I don't start eating.  It's just good not be numb for a while, and I'm going to enjoy it for as long as it lasts.

## Part II

**Delicate Men** | Colin (1981)

The first day of school and it's one of those cold ones where the sky looks like it came right out of a black & white movie. We're still unpacking, and the box with all my jackets is who knows where. So it's either my winter coat, which even I know would look ridiculous in California, or my dad's old work jacket—a navy blue, sharp-collared, cut-tight-at-the-bottom-so-it-doesn't-get-sucked-into-machinery, machinist's jacket. I go with the work jacket even though it fits all saggy in the shoulders and so long in the sleeves I have to cuff them just so my hands can make it out far enough to carry my backpack. And on top of all that, there's a patch over the heart with my dad's nickname on it, "Packy."

My mom says it will be okay, that making new friends will be tough for my little brother and sister too. But Brendan and Sheila are still in grade school, and little kids don't care what you're wearing or how you do your hair. Not like junior high, where everybody notices everything. Especially when you're new. That's why it would be a lot easier if I had my Paterson All-Stars jacket, because then the guys would all see I can play ball, and they'd probably like me right away.

When I get to school, I don't stuff the jacket in my locker like I would have back home. In southern California, everything is outside. Instead of hallways, there's breezeways, which is a nice way of saying tunnel. And you might not think it can get all that cold in California, but on a cloudy day you can keep ice cream from melting in one of those breezeways.

Right before lunch, this guy comes up to my locker and says, "Hey Packy, where you from?"

He isn't real big, but he's bigger than me, so I try to be cool about it. "Jersey."

"Jersey?" he says. "Isn't New Jersey where all the fags hang out?"

"You'd know," I say.

It's barely out of my mouth before he's got me by the collar of my jacket. "I know only a faggot would wear a jacket like this."

People around the lockers stop what they're doing and look at me like maybe I'm supposed to have some big reaction. Then someone behind me says in a real casual voice, "Knock it off, Jaime."

As this Jaime guy lets my collar go and steps back, some big guy with his hair perfectly combed so it looks kind of messed up steps around me. His shirt is this nerdy, checkered button-up that's hanging out everywhere except by the back pocket where his yellow, Velcro wallet is sticking out. You can tell it's that way on purpose, like a gun holster, like he could whip out his money real fast in case of an emergency.

He looks around at everybody, then says, "How you doing? I'm Garrett." He reaches out and flicks the patch on my jacket. "Is your name really Packy?"

"Nah. It's Colin."

"Colin?" he says. "What kind of name is that?"

Everybody laughs and I'm thinking maybe he's setting me up. "The kind my dad would give me, I guess."

Garrett gets this smirk and looks me over. "Cool jacket, man."

"You busting my chops?"

"Busting your chops?" He glances around like maybe Jaime or somebody can explain what that means, only nobody says anything. "You mean razzin' you?"

"Yeah, I guess."

"No, man. It's Fonzie cool."

"Yeah?," I say, looking around to see who's grinning and about to laugh at me. "I think it's about that old, too."

"Maybe," he says and laughs, and when Garrett laughs, everybody else starts laughing. "You're quick," he says. "You should hang with us."

"Totally," Jaime says and slaps my shoulder the way your buddies do when you make a great catch. "Sit at our table for lunch, Colin."

That's all it takes and I'm one of the guys. But just to be safe, I wear my dad's jacket to school every day.

Looking at Clifford Matlin, you'd think he could be one of the guys too. He's as big as Garrett, but he doesn't know how to use it for sports or anything. All it does is make him easier to spot in a crowd and see how weird he

is.   You see his head over everyone else's at
assemblies, his hair hanging down in his eyes
and every two seconds him pushing it over the
rim of his glasses or tucking it behind his ears.
Sometimes, he shows up to school wearing
jeans that are too long and cuffed like it's the
fifties.   Other times, he wears this big, fluffy,
turtleneck sweater with a patch that says,
*1980 Olympic Winter Games, Lake Placid.* The
patch is cool, you know, kind of sporty, but
everyone makes fun of the sweater because
who wears turtlenecks in Southern California?
And no matter how hot it is, he's always got
this red windbreaker with him, sometimes on,
sometimes tied around his waist or stuffed in
his backpack, but always there, like his mom
won't let him out of the house without it.

One day, Clifford brings this glass jar to
Pre-Algebra and hunches over it the whole
time with both hands on the lid.   Every couple
of minutes he reaches a hand out into the air
and pinches his fingers together like he's
caught something.   Then he unscrews the lid
of the jar, flicks whatever it is inside, and
screws the lid back on.   When I ask him what
he's doing he whispers, "Catching atoms for an
experiment."   Then he grins like it's some
funny joke.

I don't razz Clifford or anything when he
tells me.   Who is it going to hurt if he catches
a few atoms?   That doesn't stop other people
though.   The girl in front of me starts telling
everyone around us and in five minutes you
can see people on the other side of the room

whispering and then looking over at Clifford and giggling. By the time the bell rings, he looks kind of mad and mumbles something about Albert Einstein's teachers not understanding his genius. "Maybe his accent was too thick," somebody says, and a bunch of people laugh. Then they tell the people who haven't heard, and before you know it everyone is laughing their way out the door and not listening to a thing Clifford says.

At lunch, Jaime can't stop looking around for Clifford, wanting to see if he still has the jar. I try to act like that's stupid and we should play basketball or something like we always do, but when the guys spot Clifford sitting over by the tennis courts with the jar right next to him in the grass, they take off to razz him. And it's not like I join in or anything. I just hang back and watch him take it until Garrett says to back off because it's too easy, and what's the point of that?

When baseball season starts, I get drafted on to Garrett's team—the best team in the league. Our coach tells us second place is just a coward's way to say you lost, and he swears he'll bench anyone, even Garrett, if you miss practice for anything besides dying. But that's okay, because we can't get enough baseball. Every day at lunch Garrett gets some guys together to play *pickle*, and since I'm on his team, I'm always one of the guys.

About a week before summer vacation, we're playing *pickle* and Jaime launches the ball past me like a missile. It skips across the grass all the way over to the fence by the tennis courts. I run after it, and as I get closer I see the ball has wiped out Clifford's apple juice. He's got the ball in his hand, staring at it like it's a meteorite or something. Then he looks at me through his hair, his eyes squinty because of the sun. "I think you owe me an apple juice."

I say, "Sorry, it was an accident."

He shakes his head no and grips the ball with both hands. Everyone is waiting, so I tell him, "It's not even my ball, Cliff. It's Jaime's. If you don't give it back, he's going to get pretty mad."

Clifford ignores me and stuffs the ball in his backpack, his windbreaker all around it like a nest. He zips everything up, and just like that all the guys come over.

Jaime gets in Clifford's face, and just as he's about to rip the backpack away Garrett stops him. Garrett doesn't stick his hand out or anything; he just says, "Come on, Clifford, lunch is almost over. Give us the ball."

Clifford stares at the grass, shakes his head and mumbles, "N-no."

People who weren't even playing start coming over then, everyone making this half circle behind Garrett. Garrett asks Clifford for the ball again and gets another *no*, and you might think he's expecting that the way he lets his head drop slow and relaxed, bobbing a little on the way down, almost like he's nodding. He stares at the spot in the grass

Clifford's staring at, then raises his head back up. "You're gonna need to give that back, Cliff. Unless you're feeling lucky." Garrett crosses his arms, and they look kind of big all coiled together. "You feeling lucky, Cliff?"

We all laugh and Garrett could let it die right there, but he has the crowd. "If you can't see a ball rolling toward you, those glasses aren't doing you much good. Maybe you need a haircut. Or a guide dog."

Everybody busts up at that, even me, but it doesn't matter. Clifford still has the ball in his backpack and both hands wrapped around one of the straps. And without looking at anyone except Garrett, he says as clear as anything, "At least I don't use a pound of grease to keep my hair out of my eyes."

It's not exactly the best comeback ever, but Garrett looks pretty shocked anything came out of Clifford's mouth. "Give me the ball, Clifford. Give me the ball right now, man, say you're sorry for that little comment, and you'll get to keep existing."

Clifford shakes his head and pulls tighter on the straps of his backpack.

"Poor guy's having a meltdown," Garrett says, except nobody's laughing anymore. So with his finger an inch from Clifford's nose, Garrett says, "If you don't want to spend the rest of your life dead, you'll give me that ball right now."

"No."

"I don't want to have to fight you over this, man."

Clifford looks around at everybody and says, "Why? Are you scared of me?"

Garrett isn't scared. He can't be. But it seems like forever before he finally throws up his hands and says, "Fine, today after school. Behind the bleachers." His face is glowing, and he looks Clifford over one more time. "You better be ready," he says, then walks away.

Everyone runs out to the far edge of the football field as soon as school lets out. I'm one of the first people around the backside of the bleachers, and Clifford is there just like he said he'd be. In about a minute, a circle two or three people deep forms around him and a bunch of other people climb to the top of the bleachers to look over the back.

When Garrett finally slips through the crowd, he slaps my shoulder and says, "This will probably only take a second." He looks at me real confident, then tosses his backpack to Jaime and steps inside the circle.

Garrett lets it quiet down, looking around and taking in all the faces before stopping at Clifford's. "This is your last chance, man. Just give me the ball, say you're sorry, and we'll be cool. You won't get hurt."

Clifford stands there, his face totally blank and his hands hanging by his sides, all bunched up into fists. He stares straight ahead into nothing, and you can't tell if he's even listening.

"Well," Garrett shakes his head, "at least take off your glasses."

Clifford snatches his glasses with one hand and tosses them backwards without looking. It's amazing because the glasses don't crash down in the grass like you'd expect; they land on top of his backpack all gentle—as if he planned it that way. The one thing Clifford ever got right, and he doesn't even notice. He walks to the middle of the circle, stops, tucks some hair behind his ears, bends his knees, and brings his fists up near his eyes the way guys on TV do. It looks ridiculous because you know the only way a guy's going to win a fight with a stance like that is if he's the star of the show.

Garrett shuffles forward, steady, and puts his fists out in front of his chest. I've never seen him fight, but he sure looks like he knows what he's doing. Everyone starts cheering, calling out Garrett's name and rooting him on. But me, I don't make a sound; I just push forward a little and get on my tiptoes to see everything.

They start circling each other, waiting to see who's going to throw the first punch. Garrett looks sharp, the way you'd expect, but Clifford doesn't look scared like you might think, just focused. Then Garrett swings low, splitting Clifford's arms and catching him square in the stomach. Clifford's eyes open real wide, like he's surprised, and his hands drop. He winds up to counter-punch, but Garrett connects solid on his cheek, and he falls.

The circle explodes in cheers and guys like Jaime Muzi pump their fist the way you do when a guy hits a home run. We all know it's over because Clifford doesn't try to get up. He just lays there, doubled-over on the ground. Garrett waits a few seconds, to make sure, then he goes over to Clifford's backpack and pulls the ball out. Half of Clifford's jacket comes out too, like it didn't want to let go, and his glasses fall to the side. You might think Garret would hold the ball up all victorious, but he just sets Clifford's glasses back on top of the backpack, then walks to the edge of the circle real fast, tosses the ball to Jaime, and keeps going right through the crowd. Everyone goes after him and slaps him on the back and congratulates him like he's some kind of hero.

I wait to see if Clifford will get up, and after the last few people clear out, he does. He's holding his stomach as he walks over to gather up his stuff, and when he kneels down I see the tears streaming from his eyes. But he isn't crying. He just pulls his jacket all the way out and wipes his face with the soft, cotton part in the lining. And though you can already see the red mark where Garrett connected, Clifford doesn't make a sound. It takes him both hands to fit his glasses over his ears and then he looks up at me through that stupid hair. I want to say something, to tell him it was a good try or a lucky punch, but all I do is stare at him a few seconds until I hear someone calling my name.

Garrett's halfway across the field now, stopped and looking back at me. We're teammates, so I guess he's wondering why I'm not there congratulating him like everyone else. He calls my name again and it sounds like a question, "Colin?" All the other people shut up then and stare. I look back at Clifford who's standing now, a few feet away. I really want to say something, but I know I have the crowd, so I reach my hand out a little way towards Clifford, pinch my fingers together like I've caught an atom, and put it in my pocket. From so far away, I figure no one else can see that, but as I take off to catch up to Garrett, a few people cheer like it's the best joke ever. Like I've razzed Clifford. I don't know if Clifford understands that I don't mean it like that; I just know I've got to leave him standing there all alone.

When I get home, I go straight upstairs to my room. My chest feels tight and full and I sit down heavy on my bed. Laying back only makes it worse, like everything is overflowing into my head. So I sit up, and a little at a time I let my face go, my mouth stretching into a frown, then relaxing, then doing it again. It keeps going like this, quicker and quicker, until my eyes go squinty and the tears leak out, fast down my face and hot. It's so stupid because I'm a teenager now and I should be through with things like crying. But I can't stop. My chest pushes the tears out in heaves and with each one I make this hiss, like a tea kettle right before it starts whistling.

And though I hardly make a sound, I'm bawling like a baby.

By the time my mom comes into the room to find out why I haven't gone to baseball practice, my chest is empty and sore, and I've stopped crying. Still, she can tell, and she keeps at me, wanting to know what happened. It takes me half the night to convince both my parents that it wasn't me who'd gotten beat up. And even though they finally say okay, I don't think they believe me.

**Something Good** | Garrett (1979)

Garrett only made deals with God when he was in center field, and only between pitches. "Please let me do something good," he said aloud, far enough out into the grass that he was sure no one could hear him except, of course, God.

After his groundout in the first, Garrett was ready to compromise. "Just a single, maybe with a runner on, but nothing big, and I'll do my homework all week *before* cartoons and snack.

Three innings and a popup later, Garrett was in the outfield again. He had one more at-bat coming, in the bottom of the inning, so he reminded God, "It doesn't have to be a triple or anything. Just a little hit. Just something good. Maybe a walk. A walk and then I can steal a base."

The game was tied and with Jaime Muzi coming to the plate, Garrett took a few steps deeper into center field. He recognized Jaime by the slow, heavy steps he took to home plate, like he was sore or tired. But Garrett knew better. Jaime always waddled like an old man, then he'd explode with a big hit or a great catch. He'd already knocked in a couple runs back in the first and thrown somebody out at third. The guy always did something good.

Jaime took the first pitch for a ball and Garrett promised to take out the trash every day this week without being asked. After ball two, Garrett promised that on Monday, at recess, he wouldn't sing any of the naughty limericks Uncle Declan taught him, even the new one: "There once was a girl from Clare, whose arse was always bare..." He wouldn't even start it, no matter how much those limericks made his friends laugh, and no matter how much those friends, including Jaime Muzi, begged.

Garrett felt it was a good deal as he watched Jaime's eyes lock in on Kyle, the pitcher, daring him to throw one anywhere near the plate. But Kyle didn't. He missed high and outside for ball three and Garrett could see it now, Kyle was scared of the things Jaime could do. He'd spent the last half-inning asking everyone in the dugout if they thought Jaime would charge the mound if he hit him with a pitch. "A slow pitch," he added. "Not to hurt him or anything. Just so he doesn't hit a double or something."

At school, Garrett and Jaime were kings of four-square, working together to stay on the court all recess. When Garrett became class President for January, Jaime was his Vice President. In February, when Jaime became President, Garrett was Vice President. It was perfect until March when they ended up on different Little League teams.

"No more throwing rocks at birds," Garrett said aloud so God would know he meant it, his mind in the alley behind the liquor store, the power lines drooping with crows waiting to pick through the trash bins. Then a swing/crack/blur, all-at-once, sent Garrett sprinting to right-center, his mind catching up with his legs in time to widen the arch of his run and snare the ball on its second hop, just before it could skip past him to the fence. He spun and flung the rock hard to second, watching it sail over the cutoff man then dive for Osmar, the shortstop covering the bag. Only then did Garrett recognize what a strong throw it was, what an accurate throw, and what Jaime Muzi was doing: trying to stretch his long single into a double. But there was no getting it back now; the throw beat Jaime, Osmar's glove popping and slapping the dirt in time for Jaime's foot to slide into it like a boot. "Out!"

The second-baseman, who Garrett should have hit with a cutoff throw, gave Garrett a raised fist-pump, letting him know it was alright, that breaking the rules was okay if you got the results.

As he loped back to center field proper, Garrett tried not to notice Jaime trotting off the field. He had at least two more batters to shake the sudden tingling just beneath the surface of his cheeks. Two more outs to make sure the tingle didn't climb up to his eyes and begin leaking out. He forgot all about his deal with God, even in the bottom of the inning when he got high-fives and handshakes from his teammates, first for the throw, then for the sacrifice bunt that put the eventual winning run on second. Garrett wondered what he'd say to Jaime on Monday, if they'd even play four-square now, and if something good was ever going to happen.

## Captain of the Drive | Paige (2002)

T-Bo tells me the most powerful person in Southern California is not the governor, or a studio head, or some CEO who decides how much gas should cost. "It's the guy who's got your car keys," he says. "The valet."

We are standing in front of the Pan-Pacific Hotel, its palm tree logo twenty stories up in blue, green, and aqua neon lights. Upon the captain's hat T-Bo wears, the same logo is forged in metal—gold and matching the tassels dangling from the shoulders of his tan jacket. His khaki pants and shiny black shoes make him look like the president-slash-general-slash-dictator-for-life of some day-old African nation.

The tassels sway as T-Bo points out cars in the parking lot behind us. "If you don't have a car in Southern California," he says, "you don't exist."

I am listening because this is my first night as the most powerful person in Southern California. I'd laugh if that ridiculous logo weren't stitched to the tan polo shirt I'm wearing. If my khaki shorts and black running shoes weren't reminding me this isn't a joke. I am trapped here for the next three months—since my parents decided getting a job was a better use of time than a non-paying internship with the Anaheim Heritage and Historical Society. "The summer I drove a bakery truck," my father told me, "made me who I am."

"A computer analyst?" I said.

62

"I learned a lot about people," he said.

T-Bo warns me I'll get stiffed on occasion. "Happens to everybody. But don't take it as an insult. It's just an indication of how retarded some folks' values are—how little they know about the world they live in."

These are the kinds of things I am going to learn. A summer course in the finer points of parking cars, Professor T-Bo to lecture. This, my parents inform me, is the real world.

As T-Bo leads me to the far edge of the front drive, across lanes of red bricks interrupting the asphalt, he asks me why I think the Pan has a five-lane front drive.

I am thinking, I can connect dots; do I need to prove it? "This is a big hotel. That means a lot of cars."

"There you go." He points back towards the curb, where the valet desk sits. "Tell me about that desk."

As far as I can tell, it's actually a counter, low on the valet side and raised up high on the guest side, a place for people to come with their tickets, maybe lean against while waiting for their cars. "I guess that's where you keep the key pouches and luggage tags."

He nods. "Okay, but what else? What's it made of?"

"I don't know. Wood?"

"Oak and marble," T-Bo says, flattening his hand and smoothing the air like he's feeling the hard, cool counter as we speak. "You like it?'

I shrug. "Sure. It's nice."

"Nice? It's more than nice. It would look good *inside* don't you think?"

I don't know what to think. It's L-shaped with drawers and slots everywhere, like a Colonial roll-top. The marble does make it look important, but I really don't care where it goes.

"Why you suppose they put a desk like that *outside*?" T-Bo says.

"Because that's where valet desks go."

He rolls his eyes. "Am I wasting your time? Because you won't be wasting mine if you take a moment to think. Why is a desk *that* nice on the outside of a hotel?"

"I don't know," I say. "Maybe because it makes the hotel look more impressive. More professional."

He pokes me in the chest with a finger so big it looks like it has its own biceps. "There you go. You a professional now; don't forget that."

T-Bo points to the top of the tower, then lets his finger sweep down to the first floor. "Look at the brim of that hat." His finger traces the roof extending from the sliding-glass front doors of the hotel, over the smooth red tiles and past the bell desk, past the valet desk, reaching all the way out to the second lane of the drive. "A good hotel wears a hat with a big brim," he says. "People don't like to get wet when they get out of their car on a rainy day. A good hotel says, 'You want dry, we got dry. You want wet, we got a pool.'"

He points up and down the edges of the wide front walk to the shiny, wood-slat benches every few feet. Behind them, shrubs and flower beds surround palm trees jutting from rock formations. "Look at that landscaping. Looks like a damn rain forest."

I laugh though I do not mean to.

"But right here is the moneymaker: five lanes. You know what that does to people?" At first, he is looking at me, as if he is waiting for an answer, then his eyes drift somewhere else, seeing something I cannot see. "Confuses the hell out of them. They don't know where to go, which lane to be in. Then they see me, Captain of the Drive, and they're ready to do anything I say. Go wherever I point." His eyes return to me. "That's when you slide up with your luggage cart and as far as the guests are concerned, you an officer in Captain T-Bo's army. You got it all under control."

I nod like this all makes perfect sense. Like I care.

"That's how the Pan tips her hat to the people," T-Bo says. "And when the Pan tips her hat—"

I know where he is leading me now, and I finish the thought: "The people tip back?"

T-Bo's eyes squint into a smile. "There you go."

*

In a week, I have learned there are two types of guys who work at the Pan-Pacific Hotel, and I am neither. There are guys like Urge who never had any delusions about college and came straight to this job knowing that a valet makes a decent living and eventually becomes a captain or a bellman who makes a slightly better, decent living. He comes back from his days off talking about all the work he did on his truck, about how he can't wait until he's saved enough money for performance shocks. Then he goes and asks for tips like a caricature of a valet, almost nudging guests in the chest with his open hand: "Is there anything else I can do for you, sir?" "It's been my pleasure meeting you, madam." It's embarrassing.

The other guys are like Kennedy. Guys who think they'll be white collar someday just because they go to a community college and have heard you can transfer credits. But I know these guys. They take a couple classes a semester so their parents won't charge them rent or pressure them to grow up. Then they meet lots of other people like themselves, people who really just want to party and not think about the future. People who spend every spare second of their summer at the beach. I don't know how someone can live like that, but guys like Kennedy are more relaxed than anyone I know. And he doesn't ask for tips; he takes them. He smoothes his spiky hair and says things like, "Okay Mr. Jones, I've taken care of your car, I've tagged all your luggage, and I've got change for a twenty unless you want me to keep the whole thing." He laughs like it's a joke, to make the guest relax, but he's not kidding. I've seen Kennedy direct guests to the ATM in the lobby. I've heard him let nickels and dimes slip through his fingers and rain onto the drive, the ring of someone too cheap to give the valet a measly buck.

This is exactly what I don't want any part of. On my first two days off, I read a biography of Dr. Martin Luther King, Jr. But I didn't tell the guys that. Instead, I told them how I keep a library of books like that in the trunk of my Cavalier so my parents won't know I'm still a history major. That's the kind of thing they respect: subversion. And money. I can't talk about tips, though, about how much bank I've made, because I really don't care. I didn't take this job for the money. Urge and Kennedy disappear when a family in an old car with out-of-state plates comes limping up the drive. They know that's either a stiff or a few coins and some homemade cookies. Suddenly, Urge has paperwork to do behind the desk, Kennedy has bags to log-in at the luggage bin. T-Bo gets on them when he notices, but he doesn't always notice. That leaves me popping open hatchbacks to the scent of fast-food trash and spilt juice, heat-dried into a dizzying sweetness. Diapers, changed on the fly and not quite wrapped up well enough in plastic grocery bags. I don't mind pampering people who never get pampered; I don't even mind the stiff too much. It's the smell that makes it all so thankless.

At nine o'clock every night the fireworks across the street at Disneyland start popping and thudding over head. They bloom in reds and purples and golds, a garden of light that stops every guest at the hotel right where they stand for the next ten minutes. This is when T-Bo holds office hours. He calls people out to lane five for a scull session—to tell you to get your head on straight, or together, or to put your head together with his to solve whatever it is he called you out there for. Tonight, I am in the office. T-Bo informs me I am on probation because of my performance the first two weeks. "You got to show me more," he says. He does this without yelling, and that is the only thing that keeps me from quitting.

I can park anything. I can drive a stick-shift and give good directions to LAX, including shortcuts for rush hour. I can remember that a Japanese businessman won't kick down a Yen for lifting his suitcase, but lift a finger for a cab and it's two bucks every time. I can do everything a good valet at a good hotel needs to do, but I will not ask for a tip that is not offered. It makes me feel like I'm begging from the rich and stealing from the poor. Not exactly heroic.

"Is this your career?" T-Bo says.

"Well, I want to do a good job."

T-Bo watches the fireworks. "I didn't ask if you was committed, Paige. Is this your career?"

I can't answer. What are you supposed to say when the answer is, "No, I'm just hoping to survive the summer." Nobody wants to hear that. Especially guys who make a living doing what you can't wait to leave.

T-Bo nods, like he knows all about me. "You a college boy, right? What do you study?"

"History."

"History?" He looks me over real serious. "That going to be your career?"

I've had this discussion so many times at home, the battle of "What are you going to do with a history degree?" I'm not about to be lectured by some guy who went straight from high school to a hotel and thinks his faux Captain's hat makes him important.

I look T-Bo square in the eye. "Yeah, I'm going to get a bachelor's degree, then probably a master's. Then I'll teach, or write books, or make documentaries. Anything with history."

T-Bo nods slow and steady. "Good," he says, like he was waiting to see if I'd get the answer right. "Don't forget that."

"I won't." I say it fast, like it's the start of something more, but that's all there is.

"Then you see my concern, Paige. You got dreams, and this is just one rung on the ladder, saving money for the next semester." T-Bo pushes back his Captain's hat and dabs his forehead with a wad of napkins. That's his hanky. He looks up at the fireworks and puts the hat back on straight and tight. "But some of us, we at the top of the ladder. So you may not care for yourself, but I can't have guests thinking they can stiff anybody. Ain't no room for Chump Change James on my drive."

"But I am Chump Change James," I say.

"Then you got to find your alter-ego. Your Big Money Sonny." T-Bo still does not sound angry. "Leave Paige home with James, and let Sonny work the tips."

The fireworks crackle through a grand finale, momentarily turning night into dusk before retreating in smoke and silence. Office hours are over and T-Bo jabs me light in the ribs, sending me back to the curb. "Remember, it's always sunny when you're Sonny."

They call you by your first name around here until they respect you. It's one of those things no one ever says; it's not written down anywhere. It just is. You don't notice at first; then one day it all comes together, how a guy named Eugene, shamelessly asking for tips at any and every opportunity, became Urge. How a confident, good-looking guy named Neil, asking not what he can do for you, but what you can do for him, became Kennedy.

We do not know when or how Terence became T-Bo. It predates everyone, so he can shape the story however he wants. All he'll say is that he is the original Big Money Sonny.

From the curb on a Friday night, I watch Kennedy roll his luggage cart past a family in a mini-van for a couple in a sport utility vehicle. I figure I'm stuck with the kiddy-wagon until I see T-Bo on the passenger-side, opening the door for the mom while asking the dad, "Last name?" He fills out the valet pouch and asks where they're coming from. Then, on the sly, he asks the mom what she needs the kids to do when they get to the room: Eat? Sleep? Settle down?

She looks at him the way a guy in a Ferrari looks at a valet, wondering if he can be trusted. "Sleep, I guess."

T-Bo moves to the back of the mini-van where the two kids are touching the luggage cart, fascinated with the round, gold bars rising up on both ends, probably hoping they can ride on it. T-Bo lifts the back door, pulls out a little pink bag and says, "Whose suitcase is this?"

"Mine," the little girl says.

"And who are you?" he asks her, his voice saying, "Sit here on Uncle T-Bo's lap and tell him all about it."

"Brianna."

T-Bo sets her bag on the cart like it's filled with china. He looks at the little boy watching him from the other end. "Is this your little brother, Brianna? What's your name little brother?"

"Trevor."

While T-Bo pulls the bigger suitcases from the mini-van, he asks Brianna and Trevor what brings them to *his* hotel. They say Disneyland, because kids always do, and T-Bo frees his hands to scratch his chin. "Wait a minute." He leans over like he needs to take a better look at them, then he straightens up and says, "You're not Brianna and Trevor Ordlock are you?" Their heads bob up and down real fast and excited. T-Bo's eyes get big and round like he can't hardly believe who he's talking to. "Brianna and Trevor Ordlock from San Diego?"

They giggle and nod, eyes transfixed and wanting more of *The World According to T-Bo.* He points to an empty bench on the red tiles, the rain forest right behind it. "Not more than fifteen minutes ago, Mickey Mouse *himself* was sitting on that very bench saying, 'Where are Brianna and Trevor Ordlock?  Are they here from San Diego yet?'" T-Bo squats down eye level with them, like the biggest secret ever is coming. "Mickey told me to tell you he's sorry he couldn't wait any longer.  He's got a big day planned tomorrow, and he needed to get straight home to bed."

Brianna and Trevor nod, their eyes following T-Bo as he stands all the way back up and begins filling out luggage tags. Without looking at them, T-Bo says, "You better get right to sleep tonight.  Mickey said he'll be looking for you in the park tomorrow, bright and early."

Mrs. Ordlock takes Brianna in one hand, Trevor in the other, smiling at their smiles. Smiling at T-Bo.  Mr. Ordlock comes around the luggage cart, happy to leave T-Bo with his car, his bags, and a wad of cash.  T-Bo waves and continues filling out luggage tags as they walk away.  Then he glances to me on the curb, and I know who I'm looking at:  Big Money Sonny.

T-Bo says the only good thing about Tuesday is that it's one day closer to the weekend than Monday.  Every week it's boom and bust:  Friday through Sunday, we all make a C-note.  Whether you're a beggar like Urge or a closer like Kennedy, you go home with at least a hundred dollars.  Even I do.  On Mondays, you usually get some leftovers, and on Thursdays you get a little taste of the weekend.  But on Black Tuesday, everyone's starving for tips.

A couple hours into my shift, I'm hitting record lows: nine bucks in two hours.  Then I see this guy pull up in a tricked-out Toyota— tinted windows, racing spoiler, lowered, chrome on everything but the seats, and a thumping sound system.  I'm at his door before he's out of the car.  All he has is an overnight bag, and you don't try that Mickey Mouse stuff on people your own age, so after I get his keys I tell him, "You want to roll right out of bed and into the pool?"  I look around real fast and lower my voice a little.  "Tell the front desk you have a friend in a wheel chair stopping by; they'll set you up.  All our handicap accessible rooms are pool-side."

I give him a nod and quick grin.  That alone is worth a few bucks, and even though he nods back, all I get is, "Thanks, dude."

At first, you forget the names of people who stiff you; it usually evens out in the end.  So after the dinner rush, seeing the name Hayosh on a key pouch doesn't mean anything to me.  Not until I get out to spot F-211 and see the tricked-out Toyota.  This is good, I think, he'll hit me on the way out.  He's changed from shorts and a tee to a clubbing shirt and some pants.  I hop out of the car and say, "Looks like you got it all under control." It's the subtle way to say he's styling, and it opens things up in case he needs directions or a dinner recommendation.

"Thanks, dude," he says and climbs into the car. The door shuts and he's gone, leaving me with nothing but an empty key pouch in my hands.

T-Bo sees the whole thing and consoles me. "You went down swinging, Paige. Can't do much more than that."

An hour later, after T-Bo has gone home, I'm ready when the guy pulls up with a couple friends. It's just me and Kennedy now, and there's no way I'm giving Kennedy a chance to take credit for my work.

While I open the passenger door for his friends, I look across the roof and say, "Hayosh, right?"

He flicks his head the way people do when they expect you to know them.

I hand him the ticket as he comes around the front of the car. "Did you get that pool-side room?"

"Yeah," he says, taking the ticket and walking away without looking at me.

Kennedy sees the whole thing. "Spoiled little shit."

I park the Toyota far away, rows of empty spots between it and the next closest car. Mr. Hayosh might as well have a reason to stiff the next valet.

Kennedy's shift ends at midnight, and I've been counting the minutes. We haven't seen a car in over an hour, so he's been counting and recounting his money: 53 bucks; a ten, four fives, and twenty-three ones. "And this," he says, holding up the ten, "was for making change. 'Just give me back nine,' the guy said. Gee, only nine? Jackass."

Even though I've got just 28 bucks in my pocket, I let Kennedy have the Cadillac that pulls up two minutes before midnight. At first, I think he's in for more frustration because nobody gets out of the car. They keep the engine running and the passenger-side window rolls down as Kennedy walks up. A guy in a suit and tie asks him to kick down directions for a good strip joint. Kennedy starts talking, pointing in the air, a left here, two lights and then a right. Before the window goes up, the guy hits him with some cash and Kennedy thanks him professionally, which means without looking at the money right away. He walks back to the curb with a grin on his face, and I'm expecting him to say he sent them to a gay bar or a church. He walks past me to the ramp between the valet desk and the bell desk. The ramp leads down to the locker-rooms, like a tunnel in a stadium. Kennedy pauses a second, then he holds up a bill without looking at me and starts marching down the ramp, shaking his fist like he just won the Super Bowl.

"Made my C-note," he yells.

"You got a Grant for that?"

"Surrendered right into my hand," he says and disappears into the tunnel.

I laugh at first. Then it hits me: I probably won't make five bucks the rest of the night. But Kennedy, he made fifty in about two seconds because he knows where girls get naked.

It's maybe ten minutes after Kennedy leaves when Mr. Hayosh is back out with his friends. I bring the Toyota around and get, "Be back in a few," for my efforts. Another car comes up the drive in his taillights, a couple getting back from a night out. That's not usually a tip, and it's not this time either. I leave their car on the drive for over an hour, until I recognize the headlights of the Toyota coming through the front gate. I scramble into the couple's car and drive to the top of the parking deck, three floors up. Instead of hustling back after I've parked the car, I lean over the railing, look down at Mr. Hayosh standing by his open car door. The Pan looks lifeless with all five lanes of the front drive empty, with the graveyard bellman away from his desk and me away from mine. Mr. Hayosh keeps waiting, looking around, probably thinking he's too good to self-park.

This could go on all night and I'd wait, but then the graveyard bellman comes back from wherever he's been and scurries over to take Mr. Hayosh's keys and write him a new ticket. I return to the Toyota, annoyed as I slip inside, thinking about reprogramming all his preset radio stations. I consider stealing all the change in his ashtray, but as I slide it open I find something better: sticks of sugarless bubble gum. Kennedy says sugarless gum melts easier in the heat, especially inside a car sitting in direct sunlight. I unwrap sticks of gum and feed the

CD player as I pull onto the roof of the parking deck. By nine tomorrow morning, the inside of this car will feel like Phoenix. My name and handwriting are not on the key pouch, and with the radio tuned to a good station, Mr. Hayosh won't discover a problem tomorrow until he's on the freeway. By then, the hotel is no longer responsible for the car. "We can't control what happens off property," my manager will say. "Don't try to blame us."

I am thinking, you don't fuck with the most powerful person in Southern California. Tomorrow morning, when I go to the beach with Kennedy, I'll tell him I finally used the gum trick. He'll be proud and ask if I remembered to take the wrappers with me so only a stereo technician can piece the story together. As I walk down the ramp to the locker-room, I crinkle the wrappers into my pocket.

*

Two weeks into July, this is what I do: sleep until ten, go to the beach with Kennedy until three, come home, shower, get to work by five, get home by two, watch TV, and go to bed by three. On days off, I go to beach parties, hotel parties, house parties. I spend my money on shiny shirts and new CD's for the new sound system that's worth more than my Cavalier. I faithfully read the sports page and weather so I can talk baseball with T-Bo and tell guests things like, "Take a light jacket if you're going to be out past ten." I stand on a curb forty hours a week talking about cars and sports and girls. I laugh every time Kennedy glances at the wad of bills in my front pocket and says, "You got good bank, or are you just happy to see me?"

I have been dreading July 9th, not because it is a Wednesday night shift, but because it is the start of a baseball card convention. T-Bo says we'll get a handful of retired ball players and their agents, and they will tip well. We'll also get a few hundred collectors hoarding every last cent for some baseball card they can't afford in the first place. Chump change at best.

As they started trickling in tonight, it was exactly as T-Bo said: a dollar here, a stiff there, and I didn't see one famous ball player. Now, with the dinner rush over, it's completely dead.

I'm on the curb with Kennedy and T-Bo, watching the fireworks fizzle out as a Lincoln Continental pulls up. T-Bo steps on to the bricks and says, "Watch me turn this Abe Lincoln into an Andy Jackson." He sweeps his hand downward as if he's bringing the car to a stop (that's his move), then he opens the passenger-side door to an old man, his hair gray and thin like his body. He has those old man glasses with the huge lenses. From two lanes away, where Kennedy is giving me dating details about a girl we met at the beach, I can see how thick they are. His slacks are nice but not the tailored kind you see businessmen wearing. He probably calls them trousers. And even though it is 78 degrees with a nighttime low of 70 expected, he's worn his sport coat in the car. At first, I think it's the wrinkles making the coat look slightly off, but it's actually a lighter black than the pants.

Kennedy abandons his story and affects an old man voice, "Here you are, junior, a bright, shiny quarter for all your help."

The old man struggles out of the car, but when T-Bo offers a hand he won't have it. "I got it, young blood. It's just not as fast as it used to be."

Kennedy and I laugh because T-Bo is not a young man. He's got to be thirty-five, maybe forty; he won't tell us for sure.

As T-Bo walks to the trunk he says, "Welcome to the Pan-Pacific Hotel, gentlemen." His voice sounds like a smile. "I assume business is your pleasure?"

The driver, a white guy about T-Bo's age, pulls his own sport coat from the back seat and slips it on. "We're here for the card show."

With a suitcase in each hand, T-Bo nods and takes a quick, closer look at the old man. I do too, and he looks about as famous as the two guys who rode with Paul Revere.

The trunk is unloaded in seconds, and T-Bo shuts it smoothly, without a slam. The old man puts a hand on the cart, like he's expecting a gust of wind to knock him over. He reaches for a little brown satchel, the leather cracked and fraying at the corners. "Give me that one there."

T-Bo hands over the satchel and slides luggage tags and a pen from his pocket. "You want me to put everything under your name, Mr. Steadman?"

The old man smiles. "That'll be fine."

T-Bo gives him the usual routine about tagging the luggage and leaving it at the bell desk so it can get to the room right when Mr. Steadman does. He's also supposed to say how valet parking works. Instead, he says, "I'm going to keep this car on the curb for you, Mr. Steadman. I know you like to make fast getaways."

Mr. Steadman laughs at this and so does T-Bo. Even the white guy laughs.

"Are you watching this?" Kennedy whispers.

Mr. Steadman offers his hand to T-Bo. "You call me Shine; you hear?"

T-Bo shakes his hand slow and steady. "Name's T-Bo. And it is truly my honor to meet you, sir."

Mr. Steadman looks at him like a son, but Kennedy and I have seen this before. By the end of a shift, T-Bo's been father, son, or spiritual advisor to almost every guest he's met.

Without looking at Kennedy, I whisper, "Steadman? Shine? Who is this guy?"

Kennedy puts his arm over my shoulder and squeezes for a second. "Paige, Paige, Paige. Have I taught you nothing?"

I lean in to Kennedy just a bit and agree. "Pretty much."

"Exactly." Kennedy lowers his voice again. "He probably flashed T-Bo a couple Andy

Jacksons. Why else would you curb a Lincoln?"

Curbing a car means you leave it out front, right on the curb where everyone can see it. It makes the owner happy and the hotel look good because people who bribe valets usually drive Aston-Martins and Bentleys. And that's how you sell it too. Like a bribe. You make it sound like the curb is only for the hotel's owner, foreign dignitaries, or fire trucks.

T-Bo walks to the curb with Shine, towing the luggage cart behind him. The white guy goes on ahead, saying he'll check in. Shine starts unzipping the satchel and I know this is it. Kennedy is cool; he walks past them to retrieve a stray luggage cart—the one he always leaves out so he can stroll past guests about to kick down or good looking girls waiting for a cab.

T-Bo's eyes follow Kennedy the whole way before he realizes Shine is digging around in the satchel. "Now you know I can't take anything from you. That'd put me deeper in your debt."

Shine looks up at T-Bo and grins, then he zips up the satchel. Kennedy looks stunned as he brings the empty luggage cart back over. We watch T-Bo and Shine walk towards the glass sliding doors together. They stop at the bell desk, where T-Bo will have to take the cart back into the luggage bin. Shine tucks the satchel under his arm so he can shake T-Bo's hand again, this time with both of his, cupping it the way ambassadors do. It doesn't make the old man look frail, though; his hands are big. It's T-Bo, all smiles and too happy, who looks like a little kid.

Shine strides into the lobby, his steps now more sure, as if he's warmed up or forgotten how old he is.

"Did you see that?" Kennedy says. "Who the hell is that guy?"

"Shine."

"No," he says. "I mean the other guy."

T-Bo's grinning as he walks back to the drive, bounding along until Kennedy, safely behind the desk, stops him in lane one with, "Chump Change James! Is that you?"

I'm still at the curb, thinking there's a better explanation. "Card collector?"

T-Bo shakes his head in a parental way, like we're the ones who got stiffed. "That man doesn't collect baseball cards. He signs them."

I won't say he didn't look like anyone to me, but Kennedy is brave enough to put words to my thought. "I've never heard of anyone called Shine. Who'd he play for?"

T-Bo starts listing the teams on his fingers, "Homestead Grays, Indianapolis Clowns, Birmingham Black Barons—"

"Who?" Kennedy says.

"The Negro Leagues?" I say. "He played in the Negro Leagues?"

T-Bo steps over to the curb, taller than me even though I am on it. I suddenly feel a weight to the word "Negro," but I know I've used it properly. "What's a white boy from

Orange County know about the Negro Leagues?"

It scares me a little, and I ramble like a course catalog: "We talked about it in my American Popular Culture class. About how the league is a microcosm of the American experience."

Montgomery "Moonshine" Steadman played over twenty years in the Negro Leagues. T-Bo says they called him "Moonshine" because he ran it for his daddy growing up in Mississippi. Literally ran it. Through the woods, across farms, anywhere it was hard for cars to get and fat policemen to follow. People said that's how he got so fast and stole so many bases. Later, they just called him "Shine" so his name would be fast too.

Kennedy cannot care less. "All I know is you got stiffed."

I'm looking for the connection here, wondering why it's okay for Shine to stiff T-Bo, but he's looking off into nowhere, telling stories, talking about Shine finally getting signed to the Major Leagues. "He batted .470 in spring training for the Chicago Cubs. Then they sent him back down to the minors for talking back when some white players insulted him."

"I can't believe that," I say.

"It's a boy's game," T-Bo says without the smile in his voice, "but you got to be a man to play it."

Kennedy is not impressed. "He gave up the Majors to make a point?"

I see it now, how Shine's obscurity makes him even more memorable. "He gave it up to be a man," I say.

T-Bo slaps me on the back. "There you go."

*

Urge says I act so much like T-Bo now I should get an Academy Award. He and Kennedy called me Oscar for awhile, but the name didn't take. T-Bo wouldn't even dabble; it was "Paige, help these folks out," and "Paige, park this car." But fifteen minutes after we met Shine last night, T-Bo tossed me a key pouch and said, "Clear up my drive, Costar."

Tonight, when I got to the valet desk to start my shift, Urge came up to me and said, "Listen Costar, I'm in charge of the drive until T-Bo gets back from his dinner break."

Kennedy was over by the rain forest, planting his first luggage cart of the evening. "I'm not a costar," he yelled, "but I play one on TV."

My nametag still says Paige, but T-Bo has made it unofficially official. It doesn't matter if I like it or not; it's who I am. So I stepped behind the desk, found the list for who's up to get a car, and wrote "Costar" at the bottom.

My new name has not moved in half an hour. Kennedy is at the top of the list, and he says he has been since five minutes before my shift started. I've been waiting at the desk with him the whole time, trying to convince him his three bucks are better than the nothing I've made so far.

"Oh yeah?" Kennedy says. He holds one of the bills up. "I got this from some jackass in an old Porsche. He gets his own luggage and then says to me, 'Put my baby somewhere nice.'" I look out onto the drive; the Porsche is not there. "For a buck," Kennedy says. "I put it in a real nice spot on the deck."

I laugh. "Hold on to the dough—"

"And we'll bake it for you," Kennedy finishes.

We stop laughing as, finally, a guest arrives with a ticket. Kennedy is hand-shaking polite until he sees the name "Steadman." It's the agent. I look to the curb and see Shine already standing by the Lincoln—different color trousers, same sport coat, same brown satchel.

"Let me get this," I say.

Kennedy makes sure the agent has stepped away from the desk. "It's a stiff."

"I know."

He pulls the key pouch from the drawer and folds his arms, tucking it away. "Why do you want a stiff?"

"What does it matter? I'm at the bottom of the list."

Kennedy studies me. "Give me a buck."

"For a stiff?"

"For bumping to the top of the list."

I reach into my pocket.

"Wait a second," Kennedy says. "You're going to do it?" He looks over at Shine. "This guy flash you a fin?"

"No," I say. "Look, I'll give you whatever he gives me."

Kennedy hands me the pouch. "I'm watching, Costar. I'll go get my cart if I have to."

"You can trust me," I say.

The agent waits on the driver's side of the car, but I walk to the passenger side, by Shine. I've mastered the one-hand, unlock, unlatch and swing open. It's my move. As the door passes by, my chest goes concave like a bull fighter, my right hand coaxing danger from one side of my body to the other, my left hand sweeping behind, urging the guest into the opening.

I toss the keys over the car to the agent. "You fellas looking for lobster or ladies tonight?"

Shine reaches into the satchel, "We're fine." His hand emerges, long, skinny fingers wrapped around some bills.

"Oh no," I say.

His eyes widen, glancing to his hand and then back to me.

I shake my head, placing my left hand on the open car door next to my right, making it impossible for him to force anything on me. "Really, your money is no good here."

Shine pauses, then lowers himself into the car. I'm expecting a smile, maybe a thanks. He says nothing, just settles into the seat and tucks the satchel between his knees. The agent starts the car as I bring the door to a dull, controlled slam. I stand there at attention as the car pulls from the curb. Shine looks up at me through the glass, and I recognize the expression upon his face, the disapproval my parents reserve for class choices steeped in the history I want instead of the future they think I should have.

Kennedy is dumbfounded, unable to move from behind the desk. "I thought we kicked this feeling-guilty-about-tips thing."

I want to say it's not guilt. It isn't. I don't know exactly what it is.

Kennedy shakes his head and I know I can't talk to him about it. I wait for T-Bo, but Kennedy gets to him first, meeting him on the drive. I'm certain T-Bo will laugh in his face, tell him how little he knows about the world he lives in.

The conversation is brief, and as Kennedy walks back to the curb, his back to T-Bo, he whispers, "Sorry. I was only joking around."

"Costar," T-Bo says, turning his back, walking to lane five. "My office."

It's hours early for fireworks, so I know this can't be too serious. I walk out and stand quietly next to T-Bo as he collects his thoughts. He is staring out into the parking lot when he finally says, "Shine tried to tip you?"

I nod.

"And you wouldn't take it?"

I give him a shorter nod, to show him I know I've done the right thing.

"And when he tried a second time, you told him his money was no good here?"

"Something like that."

T-Bo turns his whole body to me, looks directly into my eyes. "What the hell were you thinking, boy?"

Suddenly, I'm not sure what I was thinking. I just know I can't stop thinking about a story T-Bo told me last night. Once, at the Polo Grounds, in an exhibition game against white Major Leaguers, Shine tagged up from second base and beat the throw from deep center field. But not the throw to third. He hit third base full stride and came all the way home, two steps to the dugout before the relay got there. As he took his third step, the umpire called him out. "I beat the throw," Shine said. "He didn't even tag me." The umpire turned his back and started sweeping off home plate. Shine's teammates jogged onto the field, knowing the futility of any argument. The shortstop brought out his glove, and when Shine refused to take it, he said he'd leave it at second base for him. 'Look, boy,' the umpire finally broke, 'you might be able to tag up and score from second in your league, but you're not doing it in mine.'

I tell T-Bo this is what I was thinking about, that I admire Shine too.

"You did like the ump," he says. "Shine played by the rules, and you broke them."

"I broke them in a good way, to show he was too good to tip."

"Uh-uh," T-Bo shakes his head. "You were showing him you'd rather have no money than a black man's."

"No," I say, then repeat it. "I did what you did."

"You can't do what I do."

"I can. I do a lot of things you do."

T-Bo walks out of his office. "You can't do this, Paige. It's not your place."

\*

I am standing on the curb next to Kennedy, a guy who will go to junior college until the day he transfers all his credits to a dead-end job with limited potential. This is not who I am.

We are watching T-Bo open the door to the Lincoln, smiles pouring out as Shine shakes his hand, says a few words, finds a few dollars in the satchel and gives them to T-Bo. This, too, is not who I am.

Later, I know, T-Bo will give me that money, the money Shine asked him to pass along. I will not argue with him and he will smile, call me Costar, and say, "There you go." I will slip the money into my pocket, be who T-Bo wants me to be. As soon as T-Bo isn't looking, I'll give that money to Kennedy like I promised, be who he wants me to be. I will go home tonight and lay the rest of my tips on the counter with my car keys. Tomorrow morning, my parents will be up before me and see how it is still July and I am already becoming the person they want me to be. But T-Bo is right; this isn't my place. The next time I have a day off I won't go to the beach or read a book, I'll go looking for an apartment near campus, a place for all the books in my trunk. I can hold out another two months, nodding, smiling, making my C-notes. And I'm pretty sure, come fall, when I quit the Pan, when my parents cut me off for not changing majors, I'll feel good about all this. Because then, I really will feel like the most powerful person in Southern California.

## Part III.
**Cards for All Occasions** | Erik (2007)

**1.1**      *Afternoon. Erik and Annie in a rental car.*

As they leave the interstate for the main highway, Annie can't get over the fields of tall grass. She's never been to California and never expected to see anything so natural and untamed just south of L.A. It almost reminds her of Kansas, she says, except the fields are more like a swollen prairie, undulating as she and Erik drive towards Laguna Canyon.

The fields fan out before them like an amphitheater, the road an aisle up the middle, leading into a canyon and then through to Laguna Beach where Erik's cousin Walter has a house and a guestroom waiting for them. Everything is five minutes from the house, Walter has said, the beach, shops, restaurants—plenty for Annie to do while Erik is at his conference. And though Erik hasn't been to the conference in three years, missing even the one in Hawaii, this year it's just a few miles from where Walter now lives. Erik will be the first in the family to see how things are really going out on the coast, the first to know if the phone calls and emails are true, that Walter, finally, is as happy as he says he is.

Five minutes down the road, the birch trees sprinkled about the fields begin grouping, inching closer to the road and clustering alongside it until the view of the hills is obstructed. A street sign suggests headlights, day or night, and the swelling hills draw closer to the road, rising until they've turned into canyon walls and the light grows shady, despite it being mid-afternoon. It stays this way for twenty minutes until with a sudden flourish the canyon walls open like curtains, giving way to red-tiled roofs, stucco walls, and the Pacific Ocean, shining and stirring like an audience on opening night.

It reminds Annie of Greece, though she's never been, and she ticks off the names of bistros, clothiers, and galleries as they drive along the coast highway. Erik takes it all in at glances, doing his best to show Annie he's listening and not the least bit distracted.

**1.2**     *The same afternoon. Erik and Annie arrive at Walter's house.*
Walter's house sits at the end of a block on a hill, a wood-sided cottage blending in with the thick brush and trees framing it, slipping into the hillside like the last piece of a puzzle. None of the houses in the neighborhood appear lavish or overdone, yet they're all manicured, tidy, perhaps too perfect.

Annie can't wait to meet Walter. She's heard so much about him from Erik, how proud everyone in the family is of his career and independence—things they never expected of the boy who was forever in Erik's shadow. They still worry for him though, being so far away, having no family around and closing in on forty and still no one special in his life.

Annie is up the walkway and almost to the door before Erik's pulled the luggage from the trunk. A man with thick black hair and a suit tailored to fit the body of an athlete opens the front door and Annie stops just short of handshake distance.

"You must be Annie," the man says with a hint of an accent, maybe Central or South American. "And Erik?" his voice carries over to the car without a yell.

Erik comes up the walkway, a suitcase in each hand, a smaller bag over his shoulder.

"I'm Junot," he says, slipping Annie's little bag from her with the deftness of a pick-pocket. "Wedge had to get over to the theater for an emergency."

Junot motions them into the house like an usher, relieving Erik of a suitcase as he passes.

"*Walter* had an emergency?" Erik says.

Junot closes the front door behind them, rolling his eyes as if they are all in on the same joke. "Somebody broke a lamp on set, so he's out scouring antique stores for the perfect replacement. Who's going to notice one little lamp, right?" He glides across the living room tiles, leaving the bags by the hallway and leading Annie and Erik into the kitchen and breakfast nook. He hands Annie a key and a scrap of paper. "This is the spare and Wedge's cell number. I'm sorry I can't stay for a bit, but I need to get back to work."

Annie is all smiles. "Are you in the play?"

Junot shakes his head, "No, not much of a call for brown boys in *Tea & Sympathy.*" He pulls on his suit jacket with both hands, pressing it to dry-cleaned perfection. "But *Night of the Iguana* is up next, and I'm perfect for that."

"Exciting," Annie says.

Erik takes the cell number from Annie. "So where do you work?"

"One of the galleries down the hill. Just part-time."

Erik nods to Junot's suit. "Armani?"

"Dior."

"No wonder actors starve."

"They would at these galleries," Junot says. "Too many *weekenders* window-shopping." He glances at his watch before stepping over to Annie and taking her hand. "If I am from Guatemala, no matter what I say about art, it is nothing. But," his voice rises into an Italian accent, "I say the same things with this Italian accent, and maybe you buy, eh? I throw in words like *Renaissance, fresco,* and," he enunciates each word with his free hand, "the brush strokes of an angel's wings. Si signorina, suddenly you are excited about my expertise, yes?" He lightly kisses Annie's hand and lets it drop.

Annie laughs and claps her hands together.

Junot takes a quick, polite bow as he backs out of the kitchen. "We've got dinner reservations at eight. Dress to impress."

Erik is tightlipped until the swish of the front door announces Junot's exit. "That was quite a performance."

"The accent was perfect," Annie says, a smile still upon her face. "He's wonderful."

**1.3**    *Late afternoon. Erik and Annie on a couch in Walter's living room.*

Erik has told Annie what it was like for Walter growing up. They were in the same year at St. Benedict's in Kansas City, but while Erik was Mr. Everything—good grades, varsity football and baseball, constant stream of girlfriends despite the fact it was an all-boys school—Walter was, at best, Mr. Everything's quiet cousin, at worst, Mr. Everything's balding cousin.

"There," Erik shows Annie in a family photo in the living room.

"My gosh," Annie says. "He looks like he could be your older brother."

"Yeah, he put on some weight junior year when I got him to go out for football and it never went away. But then I could get him to more parties and things since he was on the team."

"You really looked out for him, didn't you?" Annie squeezes Erik's arm and leans into his shoulder, even bigger and stronger now than when he was leading his high school team to a league title and run to the quarterfinals in the state playoffs. "I can't believe he didn't follow you to Mizzou."

Walter, it turned out, didn't go anywhere at first. With Erik at the University of Missouri—first to study journalism, then English, then Business when he realized he'd need a job after graduation—Walter spent a year at a community college. And when Erik came home that first winter break with stories about football games and his fraternity, girls from St. Louis, classrooms the size of theaters, Walter said only that a classmate had talked him into auditioning for a play about some aging athlete who doesn't really know who he is.

"He gets the lead in this community college production of *The Man from Clare*," Erik tells Annie, more details than she's heard before, "and suddenly he's excited about something. He transfers to Notre Dame, goes into debt big time, and never gets another lead."

"Oh no," she says.

"Yeah," Erik says, "but he made a few friends and went off to Chicago with one after graduation." She knows this part, how Erik was working his first advertising agency job in Kansas City while Walter was squeaking out a living with supporting roles and set design. She doesn't know Erik sent checks to help Walter get by, but now she understands why Walter is the absent cousin, the only member of the family she hasn't met in the ten months and three major holidays she's dated Erik. He's not the workaholic with the great set design job that the family brags about.

"Why didn't you tell me Walter's gay?" Annie says.

Erik sighs. "I don't know. I guess because I'm the only one in my family who admits it."

"They don't know?"

"I don't know what they know. They've been saying for years that he's put his career first, and now they're saying it's that he's renting a room to this struggling actor who can show him around until he meets someone special."

"But Junot *is* the someone special, isn't he?"

"I think so," Erik says.

"I can see why." Annie rises from the couch.

"You don't think he's a little young for a man closing in on forty?"

She walks around the backside of the couch and buries her fingers is Erik's hair, still thick, yet to produce a single gray. "Do you think I'm a little young for a forty year-old man?"

"Thirty-nine," Erik says and nothing more. He wants to say it's different because he doesn't look forty, that despite the reports of Walter's newfound dieting, and exercising, there's only so much you can do in a year or so. But he edits all of that out, doesn't even consider bringing up the newest material working its ways into the drama, that Junot is awfully young, awfully good looking, and awfully confident to be with someone like Walter.

Annie kisses Erik soft on the forehead. "I'm going to unpack."

"Okay," he says. "I should get some work done for the conference."

Erik begins scribbling some lines for the "Love and the Landscape" workshop he'll be attending in the morning. He left advertising after a few years and started writing greeting cards. No more stiff-faced, local actor saying, *Buy this. Call now. Come on down.* Now it was meaningful moments: a couple on a beach, palm trees and crystal blue water in the background. "Your love warms my days..." [Open to the same beach, sunset, the couple wrapped in a blanket and sitting by a fire] "And makes my nights hot."

At thirty-five, as Walter moved to California where the money was better and his set designs would see an even larger audience, Erik made an even bigger switch, to Hallmark. Just after making senior writer, he met Annie, a friend of a friend who said she was nice, fun, cute, and loyal to the company who hired her right out of college. It sounded like she'd just been waiting for him to find her.

A jiggling of keys in the door announces Walter's entrance. Annie comes down the hallway quickly and meets him on the entryway tiles. But this isn't the Walter she's seen in photos. He's wearing a leather satchel over one shoulder and his shirt isn't girdling a belly, just a subtle curve. There's even less hair than she expected because it's shaved short and tight with a smart goatee pulling her gaze downward, making her notice for the first time that Walter has the same, cool blue eyes as Erik.

Erik is up off the couch, "There he is," and in two strides hits his mark, a hug for Walter.

They step back from each other, smiles all around, and Walter says, "Sorry I wasn't here."

"Not a problem." Erik steps back and turns. "Walter, this is Annie."

Walter folds his arms as though she's walked in for an audition. "You are more gorgeous than Erik said."

Annie puts her hand out for a shake but Walter steps past the formality for a big hug and she squeezes in like they're old friends. "It's so nice to meet you, Wedge."

Walter releases her, mouth opening then drawing up into a smile.

"Yeah," Erik says. "What's with that?"

Walter leads them to the couch. "Just a nickname."

"Since when?"

"Since I started working down here." He sets his satchel down on a chair and leans on the arm.

"I thought you were the set designer."

"I am. But it's a small company, so when a production is short on people I'm *man number three* or *store clerk*. Whatever they need. Now they say I'm like that guy who showed up in the early *Star Wars* movies; the pilot who never gets more than a line or two."

"Oh, I think I remember that guy," Annie says.

"Wedge," Erik says. "His name is Wedge."

Walter smiles. "Junot's the one who started calling me that. Now everyone does."

"That's wonderful," Annie says.

"I don't know," Erik says. "You're still Walter to me."

**1.4**      *Early evening, Walter and Erik, showered and changed, sitting at the kitchen table and      sharing a bottle of wine. Annie is down the hall in the shower.*

Walter's house could be a set design. Every room has a theme and no detail has gone unnoticed.    Pillows look tossed yet somehow arranged.   They pick up colors in the throw rugs and the curtains like they were bought in several different places, years apart, yet have always gone together.   Light switches capture the era of the furniture in the rest of the room.   Even the towels he gives Annie for her shower are selected based on the bathroom she'll be using.

Erik expected this of Walter's home, not of Walter himself.   For more than a decade in Chicago, Walter never dressed like a thespian, or an artiste, or even a gay set designer, just a set designer—jeans, white sneakers and a gray T-shirt, all suitable for tearing down worlds and creating new ones.   Now he's wardrobed in cargo pants, urban assault boots and a ribbed henley, all looking too nice for work yet somehow perfect for it.   Casual yet sharp (it could go either way), and Erik cannot stop staring.   "Look at you," he says and sips his wine.   "You're totally west coast now."

"Look at you," Walter says.   "You still look twenty-five."

"So does Junot."

Walter brings the wine glass to his mouth for a beat, mock embarrassment. "He's isn't much past that."

"And that's working out?"

Walter extends his arms, ta-daaaa. "Do I look happy?"

"You look like somebody else is dressing you."

"Every morning."

Erik smiles and shakes his head. "I didn't ask for the details."

They sit quietly, more sips of wine, then Erik says, "How long did you two go out before moving in together?"

"In theater time, we dated from dress rehearsals through the run of the show, an eternity."

"Is that when he asked?" Erik says, "when the show was almost over?"

"I asked him," Walter says, "the night of the wrap party."

"You asked him," Erik confirms and Walter nods. "So what was that in real time?"

Walter hides his smile again with the wine glass. "About six weeks. The show was a bomb."

"Jeez, Walter. Don't you think that's too fast?"

Walter glances toward the hall. "How long have you been dating Annie?"

"I don't know, almost a year."

"And she's, what, twenty-eight?"

"Twenty-nine," Erik says. "But we're not living together."

"Exactly. What are *you* waiting for? And don't you dare bring the Pope into this unless you're going to tell me she's a virgin too."

Erik listens for any sound, making sure Annie isn't going to surprise them. "It's not that. I'm still learning who she is. Honestly, how well do—"

Walter holds his hand up like a crossing guard, then points to the front door. An instant later keys jiggle and Junot steps through the entryway.

Walter whispers, "I know the sound of his shoes on the steps." He bites his bottom lip, more mock embarrassment, and puts an end to the potential scene Erik is scripting.

Junot walks into the kitchen, a kiss for Walter, and gets a wine glass out for himself. Erik pours and Junot takes a sip without sitting.

"How was the gallery?" Walter says.

"Typical," Junot says. "I just need to go scrape some of the bullshit off me and I'll be ready to go. Two minutes."

Annie steps into the kitchen wearing a cocktail dress Erik has never seen. It's clingy and sparkling and Junot sweeps his hand up and down in the air, "I see what's going on here." He hands Annie the wine glass and steps around her. "Those breasts may distract boys, but I've got a *double*-breasted suit that commands attention," he says, dramatically throwing his head to where Walter and Erik stand, "from men."

Annie folds her arms, steps back, happy to play along. "Maybe you should go put that on."

"P-lease," Junot says and walks over to Walter. "It already worked once. I don't want to blind the poor man." He kisses Walter on top of the head, steps over to Annie and kisses her on the cheek, then claps his hands together in quick succession, "Two minutes everyone."

**1.5** *Night. An upscale restaurant on the cliffs overlooking the ocean. Erik and Annie on one side of a table, Junot and Walter on the other.*

Because Junot knows the maitre de, they're seated by an enormous window, the lights of the bending coastline in one corner and the darkness of the Pacific filling the rest of the picture.

"He knows everybody in town," Walter brags as the waiter delivers calamari, complements of the chef, whom Junot also knows.

Junot spoons some calamari onto Walter's plate. "So, this couple was in the gallery today and when they heard me talking in my accent they came right over to say hello. In Italian!"

Annie gasps, louder than she means to, and covers her mouth.

"I know," Junot says. He places his elbows on the table and his chin on his hands. "I told them in a low voice that my boss would only let me speak English at work. 'Si,' they understood. 'Yes. Sorry.' Then they started asking me, in English, where was I from, the south? Maybe Sicily?"

"Oh my gosh," Annie says. "Did you get caught?"

Junot wags a finger at Annie. "Oh no. I told them my mother was Italian but my father was Spanish and that's why my accent is so bastardized."

Erik leans back from his plate. "They believed that?"

"Not only did they believe it, they said, 'Yes, there's a hint of Catalan in your speech.'"

Annie laughs in a burst and Walter smiles, first to Junot, then to Erik. "He's got a story like this almost every day."

"I'll bet," Erik says.

Walter leans into Junot's ear, and suddenly Junot makes a show of lifting his elbows from the table. "I'm a mess without this man," he says, letting one hand fall to his lap, the other to Walter's.

"You guys are sweet," Annie says a places a hand on Erik's lap.

"Oh, honey," Junot says. "Don't let the sugar fool you. There's plenty of spice here."

Annie and Junot laugh together and Walter smiles. Erik sips his wine.

Dinner goes well, a chorus of delightful, uneventful moments, and the two couples walk to a pub. Along the way, Walter points out the natural foods store where they go for groceries and the trail along the cliffs he discovered when Junot got him to exchange cigarettes for stress-relieving walks. The walks turned into jogs and Walter jokes that he's now more addicted to endorphins than he ever was to nicotine.

They squeeze into the crowded pub, but there's a reserved table free for people who know the doorman and the servers, people like Junot.

Annie and Junot order cocktails. Walter orders a low-carb beer and has Erik take a sip, to prove it really does have flavor, though Erik still opts for a local microbrew.

A band steps onto a tiny stage in the corner and they look like nothing Erik and Annie have ever seen: a sun-glassed drummer in a bowling shirt; an upright bass player with a white dinner jacket; a lead guitarist, the only girl, in a miniskirt and basketball jersey; and a lead singer wearing suede shoes and silk pajamas.

"Ohhhhh," Junot says, "*The Busstop Hurricanes.* I know these guys."

"Of course you do," Erik says.

Junot tells Erik and Annie they're a punk, funk, rock-a-billy, lounge act. "The love child of Julio Iglesias and Johnny Rotten." Somehow the look, and then the sound, all blend together. All work. Junot grabs Annie's hand and turns to Erik. "We must dance."

Walter stands up.

Erik does not. "I'll keep our table," he says.

"No," Annie says. "Come dance."

Erik forces a smile. "Someone needs to watch the drinks. You go. It's okay."

And so Junot, Annie, and Walter dance for several songs while Erik sits, watching Junot sneak kisses to Walter, and when Annie catches Junot in the act, he sneaks one to her cheek, then pretends to gag. The three of them dance and laugh and check in after nearly every song to sip their drinks and offer to switch with Erik. He turns them down each time.

Not until many drinks later, midway through the band's last set, are they out the door and heading back up the hill, the music fading behind them as they walk, the light falling in shades to the pleasant darkness of residential streets.

**1.6**     *Late night.   Walter, Junot, Erik, and Annie in the living room of Walter's house.*

Moments after the front door shuts, Annie announces she's still on Kansas City time and needs to get to bed. Walter kisses her cheek, then says something about needing to be up early for Saturday morning children's theater. Junot kisses him lightly on the lips, says he's staying up a little longer and makes his way into the living room as Walter heads down the hallway. Erik follows Junot.

Junot flips on the television. "I can't possibly sleep until I know if the Dodgers beat the Giants."

"That's a great rivalry," Erik says.

Junot sits down on the couch, pats the cushion next to him. "Seat for one. No waiting."

Soon the house is quiet. The lights in the master and guest bedrooms are off and in the glow of sports highlights, Junot tells Erik, "In high school theater, I used to recite the Dodgers' stats to calm down right before going on stage. And during baseball season, I'd stand in the batter's box running my lines to stay calm at the plate."

"Did it work?" Erik says.

"Nobody calls you a theater fag when you're hitting three-fifty."

Erik acts interested in everything Junot has to say. "What else?" he says as Junot talks about high school dances, dropping out of college when he got a part in a small play in Burbank and, eventually, finding his way to the Laguna Playhouse where he met Walter. It all sounds perfect, not a missed line anywhere, and they say their goodnights after the Dodger/Giant highlights—Junot grinning with the evidence of a convincing win, Erik wondering what exactly Junot wants from Walter and how long before there's the drama of him leaving for someone younger, wealthier, or more powerful.

Erik slips into bed next to Annie. She wakes and begins rubbing his back. "You didn't introduce me as your girlfriend," she says in the dark.

"Yeah I did."

"No, you didn't. Just, 'This is Annie.'"

Erik can't remember. "Well, either way Walter knows exactly who you are."

She drapes an arm over him and squeezes. "I know. I just wish you'd be better about things like that."


**2.1** THE NEXT DAY, LATE AFTERNOON. ERIK IN THE RENTAL CAR.

The conference has gone much better than expected—complements from two different reps on the line of irreverent *Graduation Cards* Erik wrote for and managed. He felt so pleased that when he received another complement on the new line of *Stirring Blank Cards*, an idea he had to fight so hard for at first, he smiled and agreed, *Yes, they are brilliant in their simplicity.*

Erik feels rejuvenated; greeting cards really do matter. People would be astounded if they had any idea how many cards the industry sells in a year, and Erik honestly likes working for Hallmark, despite how big and impersonal other writers and representatives at the conference tried to portray it. He can write cards for all occasions. All it took that first year with the company was getting past the fact that he was expressing feelings for a person he don't know, from a person that wasn't him. Then, it was just a matter of whether he wanted to be witty or warm.

As Erik exits the freeway, afternoon is bowing to evening and he turns on the headlights long before reaching the sign that suggests it. The canyon is brilliant light and color at the top but alternating shadow and blinding sunset down on the road. At first, he thinks it's the drive that's making him anxious. Then he catches himself thinking about the return to Walter's house, to putting up with Junot's act and finding a way to make him bare his soul. It will wound Walter, Erik knows that, but aren't such dramas necessary to avoid tragedies?

He slips on his sunglasses, part of the conference gift pack, and drives a little faster than he thinks is safe.

**2.2** *Early evening. Junot and Walter on the couch in the living room, looking at a photo album. Annie lying on the floor, looking at a different photo album.*

Erik comes through the front door to photo albums and half empty martini glasses in everyone's hands. Walter and Junot say hello, in unison, and Annie gets to her knees to show Erik a photo of himself from high school football—tight pants and arms flexed as he grips a ball. "These pictures are wonderful, sweetie. Why don't you have things like this?"

Erik sets his conference tote bag down on the coffee table. "I do."

"You've never shown them to me."

Junot holds up the album Walter's been guiding him through. "Here's your reason."

It's a cast party at Notre Dame, one Erik had been in town for when Walter was a senior. It was the year a freshman from who-knows-where, Jefferson James Riley, got every single lead. And there's Erik, sitting on the arm of a couch, talking to the young Mr. Riley with his golden brown hair in perfect, tight curls and his slender body accented, oddly yet favorably, by strong, sinewy shoulders that can be seen because of the hip-for-that-year tank-top and jeans combination.

"Oh, young Mr. Riley," Walter says. "He didn't have a girlfriend or a boyfriend all year. Nobody could figure it out, and everyone was afraid to try. Except Erik."

"All I did was sit down next to him and try to get the answer everyone wanted." Erik takes the album from Junot. "Walter had a huge crush on him."

Annie moves closer to study the photo: Erik sitting at an angle on the arm of the couch, a slightly blurred Jefferson James Riley completely turned and facing Erik, and their faces close.

YOUNG MR. RILEY. (*Friendly.*) So who do you know here?

ERIK. My cousin, Walter. Do you know him?

YOUNG MR. RILEY. Everyone knows Barbara.

ERIK. Barbara?

YOUNG MR. RILEY. I guess he played a couple of old women last year, the nurse in *Romeo & Juliette* and something else. People started calling him Barbara, I think for Barbara Walters.

ERIK. Right. (*Pauses.*) So what's your story?

YOUNG MR. RILEY. (*Uncomfortably.*) Me? I don't have a story.

ERIK. No one special?

YOUNG MR. RILEY. You mean a girlfriend?

ERIK. (*Slides down onto the couch.*) I mean someone special.

YOUNG MR. RILEY. I'm not gay, if that's what you're thinking.

ERIK. (*Parental.*) Look, it doesn't matter either way. But you don't need to lie.

YOUNG MR. RILEY. (*Unconvincing.*) I'm not lying.

ERIK. Well, I'm not leaving your side tonight until we get to the truth.

Junot stands to make Erik a drink. "I thought you were the straight cousin."

Walter slides across the couch, closer to the photo album. "If this picture had been a fraction of a second later you'd see Erik shoving poor, young Mr. Riley on to the floor."

"You attacked him?" Annie says

"I didn't attack him," Erik says. "I overreacted a little, but the guy wouldn't even let me apologize. He was up and out the door before I could do anything."

Annie touches Erik's arm. "How come you never told me about this?"

Erik shuts the album and hands it to Walter. "What's to tell? I was trying to help out Walter."

"You know," Walter says, "he dropped out of school after that."

Junot returns and hands a martini to Erik. "You're a heartbreaker."

"That's not my fault," Erik says. "I was just trying to get him to be honest with himself. I didn't think he'd try to kiss me. He should have known I was straight."

Junot smiles. "Maybe it wasn't obvious."

Erik stands and picks up his tote bag. "Well, if he'd been honest with himself right away he'd have known people a little better." The room stays quiet and Erik steps to the hallway. "I've got some notes to make before dinner," he says, then exits.

**2.3**     *Night. A restaurant on the cliffs overlooking the ocean. Erik and Annie on one side of a table, Junot and Walter on the other.*

An encore of sorts: dinner in a nice restaurant, Mexican this time, overlooking the Pacific. Again, Junot knows the maitre de and they are seated by a window with a view of the ocean, dark except for a smattering of lights reflecting off the water, small craft and sailboats anchored offshore.

Annie is not speaking to Erik beyond asking for the salsa or more chips. Erik finds this ridiculous, but he's in no mood to address a subplot when this is their last night in town. Tomorrow is a half day at the conference, then right to the airport. Any frank talk he will have with Walter must be tonight.

Junot, unable to stand the quiet, launches into a soliloquy about waiters: how they're forever waiting for the thing they really want, waiting for you to finish so they can get to the party, to their lovers, to bed for their callback the next day. "But most of all," he says, grabbing Walter's hand while looking at Annie, "they're just thinking about that big tip poking around in your pocket."

Annie almost laughs and Junot lets his smile linger until she smiles back and begins to allow herself some fun.

The two couples stroll along a path on the cliffs after dinner. Junot keeps pulling Walter ahead, Annie and Erik coming around the corner a moment later to catch them mid-kiss or post caress, then Junot and Walter laughing and pulling further ahead.

At the gazebo where Annie and Erik expect to catch up with Junot and Walter, they find only a trailhead leading down the cliffs to the beach. Annie leans over the railing, looking out at the water. She points to some concentrated groups of lights shimmering miles offshore to the north. "Are those yachts?"

Erik joins her at the railing. "They're oil rigs."

"Oh," she says and falls silent for a moment. "Wedge and Junot look really happy."

"Yeah, that's quite a performance Junot's putting on."

Annie turns to him. "What does that mean?"

"It means you'd have to be blind not to see what's going on here."

"That they're in love?"

Erik turns to Annie, excited to confide in her, maybe get her help. "It's a sham. Look at

Junot, pulling Walter around like we're high school kids on some double-date. He's just earning his keep."

Annie folds her arms. "So what's it mean when you and I walk along a path overlooking the ocean, all the stars are out, and the waves are drowning out the sound of the cars back up on the road, and we've been alone for ten minutes and you haven't tried to kiss me?"

"You've been mad at me," Erik says. "I didn't think you wanted me to kiss you."

"How do you know? You haven't tried."

"Look, I'm sorry. I've been distracted by this whole thing with my cousin."

"What thing?" Annie reaches for his hands, pulling them from his sides to hers. "There's no *thing*."

"Annie?" He pulls one hand free and pushes it out toward the beach below. "It's right in front of us. Are you blind?"

"Are you?" she says.

Erik says nothing for a beat, then two.

"Erik," she says, her voice deeper and consoling, her body now pressing into his. "Why did you bring me here?"

Annie's eyes find Erik's and he can feel the spotlight, can feel that blowing his line here will ruin everything. "I trust you more than anyone in the world," he says and her eyes swallow this in, gently, urge him on. "I brought you here because you're the only person in the world who could help me with this."

Annie's lips, slightly parted for the *Yes* or the kiss she was anticipating, purse. "With what?"

"What do you think we should do?" Erik says. "I don't want Walter to get hurt."

She lets her hand drop from Erik's. "The first time you take me to see the ocean and it's to break up your cousin's relationship? That's what this is?"

"No," he says and searches to get her hands back. "I wanted it to be fun too—"

"Fun?" she says and steps away. "You're the only one managing not to have fun."

"Well, this kind of stuff isn't supposed to be fun."

"No," Annie says and starts down the path to the beach. "I guess it's not."

Walter and Junot are wading through the water, pant legs rolled up, their shoes on a rock. The beach doesn't offer much choice, only a few feet of rocks and sand from the cliff to the sea. Annie gives in immediately, Walter and Junot welcoming her to the water with smiles and little splashes.

"Come on, Erik!" Walter shouts, one arm around Junot, the other around Annie.

Erik steps atop a rock. "I'll watch the shoes."

"Let them float away," Junot shouts. "We'll go shopping on the walk home!"

Erik shakes his head in the dark. "I'll be lifeguard, then."

"He's not coming," Annie says. A swell swallows up her leg, higher than she expected and she screams, a happy surprise that makes Walter and Junot laugh.

Erik remains onshore, watching the three of them threaten to push or splash each other, though each confrontation ends in a short chase and a bear hug.

With wet legs and spotted shirts, they go to jazz night at the Laguna Hotel. Erik works his way through several pints of beer listening as Junot fills Annie's ear with stories of semi-famous actors she never knew were gay. Later, as Walter and Annie dance, Junot launches into another soliloquy, this one about Walter's work ethic. "Was he like this in high school?" Junot says and touches Erik's shoulder. "I want to know everything."

Erik obliges, hoping the facts of a self-conscious, overweight teen will make Walter less attractive. "Oh, he must have been so sweet and sad," Junot says. "I don't know if I could have made it if my parents denied what I am." Junot looks out to the dance floor, Walter stepping into the lights on cue. "He inspires me."

**2.4**    *Late night.    Walter, Junot, Erik, and Annie arrive in the living room of Walter's house.*

Annie has not spoken to Erik for nearly an hour and even now her general announcement about going to bed is directed to Walter and Junot.

"It's our last night," Erik says. "Don't you want to stay up a little longer?"

"You're on your own, sport. I'm done."

Walter says he'll make a big, farm breakfast tomorrow before they hit the road, but with egg whites and bran muffins.

Junot hugs Annie goodnight, whispering loudly, "Egg whites and bran. That's so gay."

"Hey," Walter says as he steps over and steals Annie for his goodnight hug. "You're the one who started me on that."

"I know," Junot says. "*I'm* so gay."

Walter smiles, says goodnight to Erik and follows Annie down the hall.

Junot flips on the television to a football game. "Look at this, Erik. This game is going on right now."

Erik glances at his watch. "But it's after midnight."

"Not in Hawaii," Junot says. "And you just got to love the name of that team."

Erik searches his memory for a moment, Junot nodding the whole time until Erik remembers, "The Rainbow Warriors?"

They watch the last quarter of the game drinking tequila sunrises, their conversation limited to the action on the field. As the game ends, Erik makes one last drink and Junot, politely, says "Okay, but we'll be sorry in the morning."

They watch a highlight show of all the day's games, talking about teams and rankings, Junot doing imitations of his favorite announcers. They look at other photo albums so Erik can share more of Walter's awkward high school and college moments and have pictures to prove it, the junior prom date Erik arranged for him because the girl was a field hockey player and needed a cover story too; the Halloween party where Walter dressed in lederhosen; and the last time Walter came home for Christmas, his last year in Chicago when he was a hot set designer whose best friends were props and pizza.

When one of the television highlights shows a kid from Texas A&M blowing out his knee, Erik rolls up his pant leg to show Junot several scars across his kneecap. "This is what I got for walking onto the football team at Mizzou." He kneads the skin back and forth. "Total reconstruction."

"Ouch," Junot says and turns his attention back to the television.

Erik lifts his hand away, offering the knee. "You can feel the pins."

Junot looks over to Erik. "That's okay. It weirds me out."

"It's worth it," Erik says, taking Junot's hand and pulling it over, squeezing his fingers to a point and pressing down. "Feel that?"

"Yes," Junot says.

ERIK. There's another. (*He lifts JUNOT'S hand and places it on his thigh.*) Torn quad.

JUNOT. (*Pulls his hand away.*) Okay. I get the idea.

ERIK. Do you?

JUNOT. (*Looks back toward the dark hallway.*) Yes.

ERIK. (*Lets his hand fall to JUNOT'S thigh.*) So, what do you think?

JUNOT. (*Brushes ERIK'S hand away. Stands up.*) I think we're pretty drunk. I'm going to bed.

ERIK. It's okay.

JUNOT. (*Tosses the remote control to Erik.*) I don't know exactly what you're thinking, but I'm not going to let you cause a scene.

ERIK. (*Whispers.*) I'm not trying to cause a scene.

"Fine," Junot says. "Whatever you're doing, just stop it."

ERIK. (Stands and draws close to JUNOT). You misunderstood. I'm not gay.

"I know that," Junot says, not caring to whisper. "You're jealous."

Erik's face drops. "I'm jealous? Jealous of what?"

"Of Wedge. Erik forces a mock laugh, but Junot won't hear it. "Just because you can't figure out how to be happy doesn't mean you should ruin it for him."

"I'm not trying to ruin anything," Erik says, "except your plans."

Junot says, "Because Wedge loves you so much, I'll try not to let him find out about this." He leaves the living room and disappears into the darkness of the hallway.

Erik's knees soften until he's on the couch. For the first time all evening, he feels drunk, but even with his eyes closed the room will not spin. This memory will still be with him in the morning, he realizes that immediately. He already knows it will play over and over in his mind for a long time, and he'll never get it to come out right.

**3.1**     *The following morning.     Walter
and Junot in the living room, reading the
newspaper and sipping coffee.*

Erik, disheveled, walks into the living
room.  Junot does not look up from the paper
as Walter stands and offers him some coffee.

"Thanks," Erik says and sits in a chair
across the room from Junot.

"Annie left," Walter says as he steps into
the room with a cup.  He had seen her make
the escape:  she offered no details, only that
she was taking the car and Erik would have to
get a cab.  Walter hugged her goodbye and
though he would not tell Erik, he knew it was
a real and lasting goodbye.

Erik takes the cup from Walter and sips.
"Yeah, I figured as much when I woke up and
her bags weren't in the room."

Walter sits back down on the couch next
to Junot.  "You'll work it out," he says and
tosses the sports page to Erik.  "She's a great
girl."

Erik nods and leans back in the chair
without picking up the paper.  He knows the
scores and highlights, knows nothing from last
night to now has changed.

Junot has a shift at the gallery, but when
Walter offers to drive Erik to the airport he
decides to go along for the ride and be a little
late.  "So you'll have company on the way
back."

"See why I love him?" Walter says.

"Yeah," Erik says.  "I do."

They drive through the canyon in silence, Junot watching Erik through the makeup mirror, Erik with eyes closed, knowing by time and the feel of the road when he can open his eyes to the rolling hills and freeway beyond, the canyon behind them.

At the airport, Junot hugs Erik perfunctorily, proclaiming how great it was to meet him, how eager he is to see him again soon, then slides out of the embrace and takes Erik's bags to the curb quickly, returning in a beat.

"You'll catch her," Walter says. "She's probably sitting by the gate with a story about not getting the early flight even though she tried."

"Probably," Erik says, but he knows better. "You should come home for the holidays this year." He looks at Junot. "Both of you."

Walter shakes Erik's hand for one last goodbye. "Maybe."

"Screw the critics, Wedge. You know when you're right."

Wedge opens his eyes wide and Erik nods. It's all Erik has to offer, though he feels certain he means it.

Sitting in first-class, filled with emotion he cannot begin to completely understand, Erik pulls out his pad, thinking maybe he can capture some of this and use it later. But the words do not come. Even after the first-class curtains are closed and the plane has risen through the clouds, nothing comes. Erik taps his pen on the pad, a blank slate before him, and he starts trying to believe that's what is best.

## **Bluff** | Mark (2005)

Mark only called to tell Shannon about the big fight in Atlantic City.

"What are you wearing?" she interrupted, her voice a smile.

He gave her every detail, right down to the tie he'd just gotten back from the drycleaner, the one from that messy lunch a week before where neither of them had time to eat.

Then he told her about Atlantic City.

"That's our six-month anniversary," she said.

Mark explained how much that meant to him before adding, "Les didn't know he'd have an extra ticket until today."

"Extra? I'm not invited?"

"Well, it's a fight and—"

"You think I can't appreciate a good fight?" she said. There was a long pause, unbroken until her call-waiting beeped. "Hold on."

Mark held on for ten minutes before realizing Shannon wasn't coming back; so he went to Atlantic City that weekend without calling back. He didn't see why a little fight should keep him from enjoying the big one. He even convinced himself it would be best to call Shannon after the weekend. After the excitement of the fight died down.

Saturday night, wearing the coat Shannon always said made his chest look larger than it really was, Mark bluffed big in a game of stud and won. Intoxicated by success, he risked everything he'd worked so hard for on the fight. Everything but a black, fifty-dollar chip. The chip looked sleek and serious, so he slipped it into his coat pocket for Shannon, just to show her he'd been thinking about her.

Mark's fortunes fell with the challenger in the sixth round. "He never saw it coming," said Les. All Mark knew was that he had a night of clammy stools at crowded black jack tables ahead of him. He hated that scene but was willing to endure it, determined to get back what he'd lost.

An hour later, down even further, Mark began thumbing the fifty-dollar chip in his pocket and glancing at the courtesy phones. "She can't possibly think I'm still holding on can she?"

On the ride back Sunday afternoon, somewhere near Union, New Jersey, Mark left it all up to a coin toss. But he had no coins, so he scribbled an S on one side of the fifty-dollar chip and sent it spinning.

"Tails. I'm not calling her back."

Months later, Mark liked to say he and Shannon broke up on principle. "That is, if we're officially broken up," he would always add.

When a woman from his gym asked him to dinner, he turned her down. In fact, Mark turned down everything until that December when, drunk at the office Christmas party, he snuck over to a darkened suite with the intern from NYU. She tugged at his tie, complemented his clothes, and asked if he'd care to wrinkle them. Mark drew her closer and they began kissing. Then he called her Shannon. Twice. That was one time too many, even for a girl who never allowed a relationship to outlast a semester, and she left him sitting in the dark, staring at the shoes Shannon gave him on their first and only Christmas.

That's when Mark—seven months, three weeks, and six days after the last phone call— decided to call Shannon back. It was just after three a.m., just a few steps away from the courtesy phones of that same Atlantic City casino. He'd long since deleted her from the contacts on his cell phone, but his right hand remembered her number by pattern while his left thumbed the inked-up, fifty-dollar chip in his coat pocket.

Her phone went straight to message, the message saying to try Kyle's number if it was "super important." Mark didn't know a Kyle, didn't leave a message, and didn't hang up. He gave the screen one, quick punch, bloodying the knuckle of his middle finger but getting the crack he was hoping for.

Mark set the cracked phone down at the closest table, a half-full game of roulette. Though the drive and stale, turnpike coffee had sobered him, Mark could feel the buzz of the ball in its tight orbit, blurred and chasing its tail. He pulled the inked-up, fifty-dollar chip from his pocket and carefully placed it on black, his eyes following the ball back into focus, bouncing, then snared by, "Double zero. Green."

Mark laughed. "Not even a fifty-fifty bet," he said as Shannon's chip disappeared in one grand sweep of the dealer's arm. He freed his neck from his tie, placing it onto the empty stool next to him. He then slipped out of his coat, his shoes and socks, piling everything on the stool before stepping away.

"Sir?" the dealer said, waving Mark's phone at him. "Don't you want this?"

Mark stopped but did not take even a single step back. "That's okay" he said. "It can't be fixed." He lingered a moment, then began walking again, growing more certain with every step of bare foot on carpet.

**Beginner's Guide to Brugge** | Jim (1994)

## Getting There

There are several ways to arrive in Brugge: Plane. Bus. Train. Drunk. You arrive via train from Paris, seventy-two hours removed from London, two weeks removed from L.A., and two months removed from your girlfriend.

You sleep sporadically on the train from Paris to Brussels, too tired to drink from having drank too much to sleep. On the train to Brugge, you begin glancing at your guidebook, trying to figure out where you will go, what you will do, and why exactly you are here. A girl whose backpack has a Maple Leaf sewn to it will tell you to check out some World War I battle sites. She is standing in the aisle, reaching up to the bin above her seat and stuffing books and papers into her pack. She says World War II memorials get all the crowds and somebody really should honor the original. "If you don't have the first," she says, her backpack sliding from the rack and on to one shoulder, "you never get the sequel."

You argue this point with her, the old "World War II is just a continuation of World War I" theory you heard in college too. When she starts out-reasoning you, without even having to sit down or drop her pack to do it, you tell her you don't think she's really Canadian, just some grad student from Syracuse who thinks socialism works but wouldn't dare say it around the dinner table back home. (Deep down, you know she really is Canadian, but now that you're certain you do not have a chance with her—because she is smarter and because you are American—you hit her with her worst fear, being mistaken for an American).

## City Centre

Brugge is a little-big city and therefore full of contradictions. You can safely navigate its medieval streets and buy Belgian chocolate right from the source, in fact, from any dozens of sources. Every third store is a source, but no one gives free samples. At least, not to a guy still wearing his backpack and walking from the train station to save on bus fare. You'll have that money marked for other attractions: Belgian beer, maybe a silk crocheted knickknack, and perhaps a tour of one of those World War I battle sites you suddenly feel guilted into visiting.

Despite everything you read in the guidebook, everything you hear from random Canadian girls, what you really want to do is see a windmill and eat a Belgian Waffle. That is your secret. Your hidden, clichéd, closeted secret. You are certain no one will understand such primordial motivation, so you're ready to tell anyone who asks that you're interested in Flemish history and culture even though you would have spelled Flemish with a *Ph* six months ago, before your ex-girlfriend gave you the guidebook. Before she was your ex-girlfriend. Back when the trip was for two, was only supposed to be a week, and only supposed to go as far as visiting a mutual friend studying at Oxford.

## Where to Stay

Though you are twenty-six, you choose a youth hostel on a nice, white-washed street of uniform buildings neither old nor new. You make good time on the walk—only stopping once to admire a windmill made of chocolate, then walking away quickly before anyone notices such a thing could catch your eye.

The guy at the reception desk says you just made it, that you got just about the last free bed they have. Your bed, it turns out, is actually a bottom bunk that sits amongst three other bunk beds: eight people in the room, six of them Scotsmen. (And by Scotsmen you also mean Scotswomen—four young men and two young women). The seventh person in the room, your brand new upper bunk-mate, is the Canadian girl whom you think hates you, but it's actually worse: she ignores you.

You are fine with this. It's not messy this way.

The Scotsmen do not sleep the first night. They sit out in the small garden attached to the room, speaking English in a way you do not understand, laughing in sudden crashes that come and go like a tide. At first, you lie beneath the Canadian girl and feel the five or six years you have on all of them. Then, one of the Scotsmen sneaks back into the room, pulling his backpack out from beneath the bunk across from yours. He sees your open eyes in the dark and whispers, "Did we wake ye?"

You are not certain what to say. "Here," he says and the light, comfortable weight of a wine bottle nests in the blanket atop your chest.

You wrap your fingers around the bottle. It is smooth and cool and pulls you up, out of the bunk. The Scotsman hands you two more bottles as you stand and whispers, "Carry those."

Though it is dark, you can see well enough to know you are nearly eye-level with the Canadian girl in her top bunk, and it looks as if maybe her eyes are open, staring at you. Or maybe not. Just as you lean in closer, the Scotsman stands up. "Let's go."

Out in the garden, you discover that the first bottle of wine is *your* bottle of wine. No glasses necessary. The Scots tell you all about Brugge. They've been here two days, seen and done it all, and now have to kill one more day before the tour they're part of sends a bus and takes them to Paris. One of them tells you of battle sites, poppy fields, and windmills just outside of town.

The Scotsmen glow red in the face with wine; their legs glow white from a summer under the merciful Scottish sun. The two Scotswomen speak quietly to each other, laugh at your jokes, but do not speak directly to you. You tell tales of Los Angeles, carefully editing your ex-girlfriend out of every story even if they're not as good that way.

In the grainy light of sunrise, you slip back to your bunk. The Scots remain outside, still talking, still laughing. The Canadian girl rolls on to her side. Curls of brown hair trickle down her cheeks, half her face emerging from tiny folds of pillow, and clearly you see one open, green eye.

You feel connected to her. You shared a train. You share a bunk. "Would you like to kiss?" you say.

She shuts her eye wrinkly tight and rolls away from you.

You take refuge beneath, staring up at her form—convex in the mattress—hoping sleep will soon take you, hoping she will be gone when you wake up.

**What to See**

In the even light of late morning, your room appears cramped with dirty clothes and backpacks peeking out from under bunks, leaning against and over bedposts, and partially blocking every route to the door. The Scots are still asleep when the Canadian girl steps into the room. Her hair is wet and she is dressed for the day: long, brown pants with zippers everywhere, even in places that have nothing to do with body parts; a gray T-shirt, the word *Roots* across her chest, the first *o* and the *t* curving out slightly. You suddenly realize this means you are staring, but it does not matter now, so you keep staring.

She does not look at you when she says, "If you're going to stay another day, you better go tell them."

You nod and feel around under your bunk for sandals.

The Canadian girl grabs her daypack and jacket and opens the door again. "You missed the free breakfast," she says.

"Yeah?" you say, the remnants of wine sour on your mind. "Maybe tomorrow."

She looks at you as though you have insulted her cooking. "Maybe," she says and lets the closing door follow her out.

## Getting Around

Because of the gray haze and misty air, the bicycle rental shop is empty when you arrive. The quiet man behind the counter opens a map. With a pen, he circles where in the grid of Brugge you are. It is a maze of canals and curving roads; three, four, and five-way stops; street names that change arbitrarily, sometimes reappearing a few intersections later.

The shop bell rings as a young man in shorts and a windbreaker steps into the store. He busies himself looking over and past you at the terms of rental posted on the wall behind the counter.

You tap the map and in a quiet voice, so it does not sound like a whisper, say, "Windmills?"

The clerk draws a line through the town, out to a canal, alongside it for a few inches, and then draws a crude windmill on the map and circles it. "Forty-five minutes," he says. "Thirty, if you ride hard."

"Are you going to make that ride?" you hear another voice say. It is the young man in the shorts and windbreaker. He is standing beside you, staring at the windmill.

"I think so." You fold the map quickly, the way you did at eighteen when you first bought a dirty magazine and the clerk asked if you were sure that was the one you wanted.

The young man looks outside. "I've been waiting to see if it would clear up," he says. "This is my only day here."

"It's not so bad," the clerk says and you know there's no getting out of this now; you have a companion for the day.

Of course, you were supposed to have a companion every day. Even after the breakup, you thought it might be exotic strangers who knew lots of secrets about the world. Or exotic women who were worldly and knowing.

Clark is shorter than you, and this makes you feel somewhat better, like you could take him in a fight, though you can see, even through his windbreaker, that his chest is more developed—not in that hulking, compensatory way, but proportional to his body.

You'd have guessed Clark from the Northeast before he spoke, before you noticed his *Colgate Lacrosse* t-shirt. His blue windbreaker brings out the slight, blue stripe on his gray hiking boots. His lean, athletic legs disappear into cargo shorts that are too short to be stylish, too long to be completely out of fashion. His mussy hair is not like the mussy hair of the Scotsmen; it is sandy, both blonde and brown, possibly highlighted, and mussed rather precisely.

Outside, you discover Clark's *Colgate Lacrosse* t-shirt is actually a gift from a friend. "I play, but at Holy Cross," he says. "We have some funny t-shirts that say 'Holy Crosse!'"

You nod and smile but the laugh does not come. "I should have one," he says and stares at the bikes. "I don't know why I don't. I guess because it was a fundraiser and it didn't make sense to buy a t-shirt from yourself."

"Did you buy one for your friend at Colgate?"

"I should have," Clark says and shakes his head. "I can't believe I didn't."

## Sights Outside Brugge

The white-washed buildings of residential Brugge give way quickly to open spaces, more trees and wider roads running along the edge of town. A pedestrian bridge funnels you on to a trail running alongside the canal from the map. Clark rides in front of you with smooth, long strokes, the bike surging ever forward, the back tire fanning water out behind and misting your face even more than the air. You try not to think of the World War I battle sites you could be visiting, all those gravestones waiting for just a moment of your time; try to reason that it's best to visit them on a clear day when you can really take it all in; and try not to feel guilty.

Later, through the gunmetal gray of the horizon, a windmill emerges slowly, like a pencil sketch, the lines growing more distinct as you push on. When you are nearly upon it, you realize it is on the opposite side of the canal and you must ride past it, hoping for a footbridge.

It takes maybe ten more minutes to arrive at the bridge. The windmill has slipped back into the gray and there is a sign for a town just a few kilometers further.

"You hungry?" Clark says. "We can ride on to that town to see what they've got, then hit the windmill on the way back."

Clark does not look directly at you as he says this. You are older and more experienced than Clark, and you suddenly see yourself in a quiet café, a plate of something in front of you, and neither you nor Clark speaking. But you're hungry. You missed breakfast because the Canadian girl did not have the decency to wake you. Lunch was not part of the plan, however. Windmills. That was it. But it would be nice to eat with a person and not your guidebook for once. That was how it was supposed to be.

"Yeah," you say. "Let's grab something."

## Where to Eat

Many of the restaurants have A-frame signs on the sidewalk out front, daily specials chalked in a rainbow of colors—most boldly saying what you are thinking: Belgian Waffles. It's as if the locals are saying, "It's okay; we know why you're here."

Clark stops his bicycle out front of a hotel cafe and laughs at the sign. "I hadn't even thought of that." His look is little kid mischief—playing ball in the house, spying on the neighbor through the fence. "Should we get a waffle? We are in Belgium."

The cold air and lack of sun make it feel like morning has lasted all day. This is the excuse you use to say *Yes* to Clark and go inside.

The waffles come with almost anything; they can be breakfast, lunch, dinner, or dessert. You both order the waffles with a side of ham, plus a beer. That makes it seem more like lunch, a more casual meal.

Your wet hair drips in soft taps on the table. "You're soaked," Clark says. "How come I'm not?"

"I think it's from your back tire," you say.

After the waitress takes your order to the kitchen, the café is empty. Clark leans over to the next table and grabs the neatly folded cloth napkin nearest him, leaving the silverware behind. "Here," he says and tosses the napkin so it hits you gently in the chest. "Hurry, before she catches us."

You smile and dry off, tossing the wet cloth beneath the table just before the waitress returns with the waffles and beer. This is a union you wouldn't dare think of back home, much less ask for, yet it seems to work. The waffle is sweet, even without syrup, and would quickly dull your taste buds if the salty ham were not there to shock them back to life. The beer smoothes everything over, makes everything agreeable, and you soon find yourself over an empty plate describing your rent-controlled apartment in Santa Monica.

"So you live five minutes from the beach," Clark says, "and you never go?"

"Yeah," you say to yourself. "Why don't I go?"

Clark leans forward, elbows on the table. "I know why. Because you can't always see how good you've got it. At least, not while it's right in front of you."

"That's a cliché."

Clark picks up his beer. "Of course it is. Because it's so true." When you do not immediately respond, he takes a swig from the nearly empty bottle and sets it on the table with a pop.

**Rare Sights**

You must ride hard to the windmill. The rain has picked up, the drops now stinging your face. When you look up to see how far down the path the windmill is, a raindrop thumps your right eye like a flick from a finger. Your contact lens lifts and slides to a corner of your eye, blurring half your world. To stay focused, you close that eye and stare only as far as Clark's back tire until you reach the windmill.

It feels warm inside, and you do not care that the windmill is nothing more than a grindstone for grains. Deep down you knew that; you think maybe you learned it in the third grade. Yet, from a distance, the windmill seemed so majestic.

You are drying and warming and just inside the door before leaving Clark says, "Is something wrong with your eye?"

"My contact."

"Oh," he steps closer. "I hate that."

You nod even though you've only had the contacts a few months, the last good thing your ex-girlfriend got you to do.

"Want me to see if I can get it?" Clark says, now looking into your eyes one at a time.

You look him over with the good eye.

"I had a roommate," he says. "I've done this before."

Clark tells you to close the good eye. Through the bad one you see his blurry face, not far from yours. His hands, warm despite how wet you both still are, lightly rest upon your cheek and forehead while his fingers, firm like a good mother's, spread open your eye. "Look up. Now down. Left." You feel a scratch with each change in direction. "There it is; don't move." Briefly, Clark's fingers fill your vision. It does not sting or poke. There is a moment of pressure, and then your eye feels washed over, as tough someone has draped a silk sheet across it.

You blink a few times before Clark comes into focus, staring into your eye. Concerned. "Did that get it?"

"I think so," you say, studying Clark's eyes, brown with chips of black and green. You blink twice. "Yeah, it's good. Thanks."

## Off the Beaten Path

You get back to town just after three. With the hostel still closed for cleaning, Clark points up the lifeless street to a pub. "Maybe we should kill some time and grab another beer."

The televisions are all tuned to a World Cup soccer match, the way they have been everywhere you've gone since arriving in Europe. Though the pub looks empty and Belgium is not in the match, the bartender takes little notice of you, pouring two pints and taking your money with little more than a glance from the television.

The beer and gradual rhythm of soccer tire you. You could fall asleep if the front of the pub, a series of glass-paned French doors, were not wide open to the street, forcing you to dry slowly in a damp breeze.

Clark says little. You say even less, the occasional, *Yep* to his occasional, *Nice play.*

At halftime, on the way back from the toilette, you notice the pub has a loft. You tell Clark it's probably warmer up there, so you each grab another pint and Clark follows you up the stairs.

The loft is simple, a long counter along the railing, empty chairs neatly lined up against it, a row of booths against the back wall, and an aisle between. Three booths in, you see sneakers sticking out, four pairs, two pair to each side of the booth. A few steps further you see the two couples connected to the sneakers, a boy and a girl on each side, lying down in the booth and intertwined, their heads perking up to stare as you walk by. And they really are boys and girls, maybe thirteen or fourteen, making out in a bar in the middle of the afternoon.

As you make your way to the far end and sit in a chair along the railing, you wonder if Clark thinks you knew the loft is a make-out spot. He sits down next to you. The teenagers are no longer visible, except for their feet. "Should we go back down?" you whisper.

Clark is grinning and whispers. "It's probably okay. They'll forget about us in a minute."

You shake your head. "They look like seventh-graders."

Clark nods and sips his beer, keeping his eyes on you. "I grew up in the wrong country," he says, no longer whispering.

You laugh, notice how Clark's eyes do not yet wrinkle when he smiles, and let your voice go back to normal as well. "Me too."

"How's the eye?"

"Good," you say as his hand finds your cheek. You open your eye wider, turn your head a little to show him, but Clark softly directs your face back square with his.

You tilt your head, breaking contact with Clark's hand, and look past him to the booth with the kids.

"They don't care," he says. "We're in Brugge. Who do we know in Brugge?"

He leans in closer and you close your eyes, feel his lips on yours, taste the beer on his breath. His face does not scratch you the way you may have thought. When his tongue flicks the roof of your mouth, searching, you realize your tongue is drawn down and back, a hollow mouth.

"I'm sorry," you say in retreat.

Clark's eyes look sleepy and intent. "It's okay."

"No," you say. "It's not." You look down to the bartender, still focused on the television, then over at the booth. You whisper: "I'm not gay."

Clark's eyes never leave you. "Back home, neither am I." He smiles and sips his beer.

You follow his lead and sip your beer, the bubbles tingling your mouth with cleansing alcohol. "I'm not gay," you say, your whisper now rising to conversational tone. "Anywhere."

"Okay," Clark says, the smile wiped from his mouth, his eyes open and understanding. "Nothing has to happen."

"Exactly," you say. "Nothing did happen."

Clark nods and turns his head to the television. You do the same, try to pretend it's just you and a buddy watching a game, but you don't even understand the rules, and you don't have a buddy who's ever tried to kiss you. A buddy, you keep turning over in your mind, who you *let* kiss you.

"I'm sorry," you say. "I better go."

Clark allows you to stand, to slip away or storm off, whichever you need to do.

You say "sorry" again, and this gets Clark to look up at you.

He says you don't need to keep apologizing, that you've done nothing wrong, and for the first time all day, he calls you by your name, the first time you've heard anyone besides a customs official say it in weeks, and it does not sound right. This is not who you are. So you slide past him, between his chair and the booth, and walk with purpose down the stairs and out the door. A calm, controlled getaway.

## Getting away

You head directly to the room for your backpack and passport. The Scots are already there, preparing for a last, big night in Brugge: dinner, wine, dancing. They suggest you put on something dry and come along. When you hedge, they insist.

Over dinner, you share the details of your day, admit you ate waffles and saw a windmill, but you share these details as though you spent the day alone.

Much wine and many beers later, you find yourself in a club, dancing with one of the Scotswomen. She's telling you how much she loves your accent, how boring Scotsmen are, how exciting it must be to live in Los Angeles. Her voice blends with the music; her head nods every time you ask if she wants to keep dancing.

When you walk her back to the table, the other Scots take little notice of you both. "I'll be right back," you say and glance toward the toilette.

She grabs your arm. "We can go back to the room if you want. My friends will be here for hours."

You understand her completely. It is not late, just after nine, and the room will probably be empty. "Give me one second," you say.

You blend into the crowd on the way to the toilette then double-back, walking around to the other side of the club, avoiding the light of the dance floor, allowing the pulse of the music to push you out the front doors.

The fresh air explodes around you as if you've broken through the surface of the water. You walk the streets of Brugge, the whitewash still glowing from the late-setting sun, the approaching night scribbling purple across an orange sky. On the way to the hostel, you try not to think, try to make yourself notice details in darkened shop windows. You count how many cars are American-made and how many of those you've actually seen back home where, long after you're asleep, your ex-girlfriend will be out clubbing with the friend who stopped being nice to you following the split

The lobby of the hostel is dark, everyone out or in for the night. Everyone except a single figure slumped in a chair. The Canadian girl. She looks asleep as you crouch in front of her. "Hey," you nudge her awake. "Are you sleeping out here?"

Her head rolls to life. "Hey," she says, her eyes closing as she speaks. "What've you been up to?"

The alcohol reaches you with the words. "Same thing as you."

"Mmm," she says, her mouth dropping slightly open after she's said it.

"Hey," you nudge her again. "You don't want to sleep out here."

She opens her eyes, "Are you afraid someone will get me?"

"I don't know. I guess."

She holds her arms forward without looking at you. "Then get me."

You reach forward and she slides into your arms sideways, wraps her arms around your neck and leans her head on your shoulder as you cradle her to the room. "I hate you," she says.

"I know."

The room is dark and empty, and she blindly reaches for the light switch.

"Don't," you say. "I don't want them."

You step over to the top bunk and let her go. She spreads out over the blanket, then grabs for your shirt. You catch her hand, lace your fingers through hers, and push her back, softly, onto the bed. "Ask me," you say.

"Ask you what?"

"If I want to kiss."

Her head raises, eyes opening and catching just a little light. "Do you want to kiss?" she whispers.

"Not until after," you say, climbing onto the bunk, feeling your way past all the zippers that don't matter, to the only one that does. "I want to do something for you first."

She watches you slip off her pants, watches as you lower your head before her, and breathes, "Yes."

You find yourself slipping into the rhythm you had with your ex-girlfriend, but the Canadian girl does not respond in the same ways. You don't know if she is too drunk or if you are a bad lover, but when she finally tugs at your shoulders you know she has given up on you.

She says it's okay, that she appreciates the effort, and she proves this to you by returning the favor, though her mouth is too soft, too hollow, and you've had too much to drink. In the end, she crawls back up to you and uses her hand. "Like that," she keeps checking and re-checking, her breath stale with alcohol. And when, finally, it is time, you begin kissing her until the warmth spreads across her hand and she sighs in your mouth, breaks off the kiss and whispers, "There you go."

After a few more kisses and her promise to wake you for breakfast, you slip down to your bunk and see her form relax into sleep above you. Hours later, as the Scots return, you close your eyes and feign sleep. You hear one Scotswoman tell the other, "See, he just came back and passed out."

When they have all settled into their bunks, settled into the open-mouthed sleep of the drunk, you stuff everything you can feel in the darkness into your pack. You carry your sandals, knowing bare feet are quieter, and slip out the door.

In the morning, the Scots will wonder where you are and if you've gone. The Canadian girl will realize that she never caught your name, that she only knows you as the ugly American. She may wonder who exactly you are, and as you sit aboard the first train to Amsterdam, promising yourself nothing but battlefields and museums from now on, you try not to wonder this too.

## About the Author

R Dean Johnson grew up in Southern California, where everyone still calls him Rob, Bobby, or Bob. Which he likes. He lives in Kentucky with his wife, the writer Julie Hensley, and their two children. An Associate Professor at Eastern Kentucky University, he teaches fiction and creative nonfiction in EKU's low residency MFA in creative writing program, the Bluegrass Writers Studio. His essays and stories have appeared in several national literary journals, including *Ascent, Hayden's Ferry Review, Louisville Review, Natural Bridge, New Orleans Review, Ruminate, Santa Clara Review, Slice,* and *The Southern Review.*

For more information about the author, this book, appearances, and current projects, visit www.rdeanwriter.com.

## Acknowledgements

Sincere thanks to the many people who have influenced these stories or touched my writing in indirect yet no less important ways:

Julie, Boyd, and Maeve for making sure writing is only one part of my life.

My parents, Kathleen and Robert, and in-laws, Joy and Mike Hensley, for the support they give in so many ways.

Kim, Jay, and The McQ's for being there when I needed it, sometimes when I wasn't even sure what I needed.

Nelson Lowhim and the team at Alternative Book Press for their belief and hard work.

Jim Saunders and Dave Long for writerly encouragement and literary direction. Toan Nguyen for keeping me grounded. Dave Andrade for saving my literary life that fall in Kansas. And to my big, little brother at K-State and still, Aaron Marshall.

Chris Cokinos, Steve Heller, Lex Williford, Mike McNally, and Ron Carlson for guiding my hand early on.

Everyone in Creative Writing at Arizona State, especially Boyd Jorden, Kate Petersen, and Jennifer Spiegel, who made me better and made it fun.

Friends and colleagues, past and present, who have been especially helpful, or encouraging, or both: Miles Waggoner, Melanie Bishop, John Morris, Ron Kates, Young Smith, Nancy Jensen, and Derek Nikitas.

The many coffeehouses that let me escape to the odd solitude of a public space where I could sit and work for much longer than my vanilla latte really earned, especially Gold Bar in Tempe, AZ; Prescott Coffee Roasters in Prescott, AZ; and Purdy's Coffee Company in Richmond, KY.

And for advice on everything from line editing to fatherhood, Kenny Cook.

There are so many more people who deserve thanks. I cannot name you all, and I won't add, "But you know who you are." Instead, let's just say that when next we see each other, I owe you a pint, and not the cheap stuff.

-RDJ

———

Earlier versions of these stories appeared in the following journals and anthologies. I am so grateful to the readers and editors who first gave these stories a platform and, often, provided astute editing suggestions as well:

"No Better" (as "Outside the Palace") in *Atticus Review* and (as "Concrete") in *Liars' League – NYC*; "The People We Were" in *New Orleans Review*; "Delicate Men" (as "Catching Atoms") in *Ruminate, Confessions: Fact or Fiction Anthology*, and *Cold Shoulders, Evil Eyes, Steadying Glances & Warm Embraces Anthology*.; "Something Good" in *Coe Review*; "Captain of the Drive" in *Santa Clara Review*, *Workplace Anthology*, and (as "The Finer Points of Parking Cars") in *Worker's Write*; "Cards for All Occasions" in *WIPs: Works (of Fiction) in Progress*; "Bluff" in *Paradigm* and *Paradigm Vol. 1*; and "Beginner's Guide to Brugge" in *Juked*.

**For more books like this from exciting new authors visit**
**www.alternativebookpress.com**

**To get book deals on authors like this one and more, sign up here:**
http://eepurl.com/Y_l6n

Made in the USA
Monee, IL
05 October 2022

15307784R00085